Quick Study

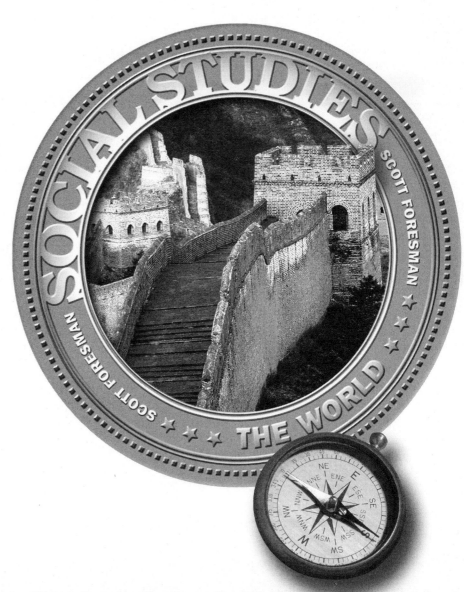

SOCIAL STUDIES

SCOTT FORESMAN

SCOTT FORESMAN

THE WORLD

PEARSON

Scott
Foresman

Editorial Offices: Glenview, Illinois • Parsippany, New Jersey • New York, New York
Sales Offices: Parsippany, New Jersey • Duluth, Georgia • Glenview, Illinois •
Coppell, Texas • Ontario, California • Mesa, Arizona

www.sfsocialstudies.com

Program Authors

Dr. Candy Dawson Boyd
Professor, School of Education
Director of Reading Programs
St. Mary's College
Moraga, California

Dr. Geneva Gay
Professor of Education
University of Washington
Seattle, Washington

Rita Geiger
Director of Social Studies and
    Foreign Languages
Norman Public Schools
Norman, Oklahoma

Dr. James B. Kracht
Associate Dean for
    Undergraduate Programs
    and Teacher Education
College of Education
Texas A&M University
College Station, Texas

Dr. Valerie Ooka Pang
Professor of Teacher Education
San Diego State University
San Diego, California

Dr. C. Frederick Risinger
Director, Professional
    Development and Social
    Studies Education
Indiana University
Bloomington, Indiana

Sara Miranda Sanchez
Elementary and Early
    Childhood Curriculum
    Coordinator
Albuquerque Public Schools
Albuquerque, New Mexico

Contributing Authors

Dr. Carol Berkin
Professor of History
Baruch College and the
    Graduate Center
The City University of New York
New York, New York

Lee A. Chase
Staff Development Specialist
Chesterfield County
    Public Schools
Chesterfield County, Virginia

Dr. Jim Cummins
Professor of Curriculum
Ontario Institute for Studies
    in Education
University of Toronto
Toronto, Canada

Dr. Allen D. Glenn
Professor and Dean Emeritus
Curriculum and Instruction
College of Education
University of Washington
Seattle, Washington

Dr. Carole L. Hahn
Professor, Educational Studies
Emory University
Atlanta, Georgia

Dr. M. Gail Hickey
Professor of Education
Indiana University-Purdue
    University
Fort Wayne, Indiana

Dr. Bonnie Meszaros
Associate Director
Center for Economic Education
    and Entrepreneurship
University of Delaware
Newark, Delaware

ISBN 0-328-09008-5

10 11 12 13 14 15 -V016- 16 15 14 13

© Scott Foresman 6

Contents

© Scott Foresman 6

Name _____ Date _____

Lesson 1: Early Gatherers and Hunters

Vocabulary

prehistory the period of time before people developed systems of writing and written language

archaeology the study of past cultures through the things they left behind

archaeologist a scientist who uncovers and studies past cultures

artifact an object made by a person long ago

migrate to move from one area to another

glacier a huge ice sheet

Studying Prehistory

Prehistory is the period of time before people developed a system of writing and written language. Prehistoric people did not leave behind books or other writings. They left other objects. **Artifacts** are objects such as tools, weapons, pottery, or jewelry that were made by early peoples. Artifacts may tell us whether early people hunted or what tools they used. Artifacts may also show us what early people used from their environment. **Archaeology** is the study of past cultures. An **archaeologist** is a scientist who studies the ways of life of early people. Archaeologists study artifacts.

Early Peoples

Archaeologists and historians (people who study history) believe that early peoples lived in East Africa about 3.5 million years ago. They also believe that groups of people began to move, or **migrate,** from East Africa to Europe and Asia thousands of years ago. Archaeologists and historians began to question who the first Americans were, where they came from, and how they migrated to the Americas.

Early Americans

Earth was in an Ice Age from about 1.6 million years ago until about 10,000 years ago. Huge ice sheets called **glaciers** covered large areas of land. When temperatures rose, the glaciers began to shrink. Land underneath the glaciers was uncovered. Plants and animals could live on this land. About 70 years ago, archaeologists found objects made by early humans near Clovis, New Mexico. These artifacts, including stone points called Clovis points, are thought to be about 11,000 years old.

A Migration Path

During the Ice Age, the seas were lower than they are today. A large area of land called Beringia was uncovered. Beringia stretched from Asia to North America. This formed a "land bridge" between the two continents. Animals were able to migrate between Asia and North America. Archaeologists think that more than 11,500 years ago hunters followed herds of animals across the land bridge into the Americas.

Different Paths

For years, scientists believed that the Clovis people of 11,000 years ago were the First Americans. Then 20 years ago, archaeologists found even older artifacts in Monte Verde, Chile. These artifacts were about 12,500 years old. Many scientists did not believe that this date was correct. It meant that the First Americans came to North America 1,000 years earlier than scientists had thought. Archaeologists discovered tools that were as much as 18,000 years old at the Topper site in South Carolina.

Quick Study

Lesson 1: Review

1. ⟳ **Sequence** The following events are not in chronological order. List them in the correct order.

_____ Clovis points are found in New Mexico.

_____ Ice Age begins.

_____ Pre-Clovis artifacts are found near Monte Verde, Chile.

_____ People migrate from Asia to North America.

2. What is an archaeologist?

_____

_____

_____

3. How do we know about the people who lived in Clovis years ago?

_____

_____

_____

4. How do we use artifacts to learn about early people and cultures?

_____

_____

_____

5. **Critical Thinking:** *Evaluate Information* Do we know for certain who the First Americans were? Explain your answer.

_____

_____

_____

Lesson 2: Early Farmers

Vocabulary

technology the way in which humans produce the items they use

domesticate to tame wild animals or cultivate plants for human use

harvest to gather crops

excavation site where archaeologists dig up artifacts

agriculture the raising of plants and animals for human use

surplus an extra supply

nomad a person who travels from place to place

social division the different roles that people have in a society

climate average weather conditions in an area over a long period of time

carbon dating a method of judging the age of things that lived long ago

The Stone Age

The Stone Age was a prehistoric time when people used mostly stone tools. The Stone Age is divided into two periods: the Old Stone Age and the New Stone Age. The Old Stone Age lasted a long time. Little progress was made in **technology.** Technology is the way humans produce the items they use. People used mostly stone tools, but they also used wood, horn, antler, and bone tools. During the New Stone Age, humans greatly improved their technology in a shorter period of time. People began using polished rock as a tool. Humans began to farm. They also started to **domesticate,** or tame, wild animals.

Early Farming

Grains were among the first plants humans farmed. Artifacts found in **excavation sites** tell archaeologists about the crops that were **harvested,** or gathered.

Domestic Animals

People began domesticating wild animals about 10,000 years ago. Some animals were used for food, clothing, and shelter. Stronger animals, such as cattle, were used for plowing fields. In this way, domesticated cattle helped **agriculture** develop. Agriculture is the raising of plants and animals for human use. Families were now able to raise more crops than they needed. They could sell the **surplus,** or the extra supply.

More Useful Creatures

Nomads were people who migrated from place to place. They domesticated animals such as horses, donkeys, and camels. These animals helped them travel great distances.

Village Life

Skara Brae was a typical Stone Age village. Some people in the village were farmers and herders. Others were toolmakers. Still others harvested fish and shellfish. Because of the food surplus, the village was able to divide up the work. This formed **social divisions,** or different roles given to different people in a society. Their lifestyle changed from hunting and gathering to farming.

The Iceman

Archaeologists also study how early people lived in different **climates.** In 1991 people found the frozen body of a man in Europe. Archaeologists studied the Iceman's copper ax and stone knife. They believe he lived during or after the New Stone Age. Archaeologists knew that copper was used during the New Stone Age. They also used a method called **carbon dating** to help them judge how old the man was. He lived about 5,300 years ago.

Lesson 2: Review

1. ⟳ **Sequence** The following events are not in the correct order. List them in the correct chronological order.

_____ Domesticated crops

_____ Social divisions within a community

_____ Production of surplus food

_____ Domesticated animals

_____ Technology improves

2. What characteristics defined the Stone Age?

_____

_____

_____

3. What is domestication?

_____

_____

_____

4. How did farming crops and raising animals change how people lived? Use the terms **social division** and **agriculture** in your answer.

_____

_____

_____

5. **Critical Thinking:** *Make Inferences* How can we know what animals Stone Age people domesticated?

_____

_____

_____

Lesson 3: Developing Cultures

Vocabulary

culture the way in which individuals and groups react to their environment
anthropology the study of how people live and develop in their culture
landform a surface feature of Earth such as a mountain or hill
geography the study of the relationship between physical features, climate, and people
diverse different

Contacting Cultures

Culture is the way people react to their environment. It includes a people's technology, customs, beliefs, and art. **Anthropology** is the study of how people live and develop in their culture. Cultures are affected by climate, plants, animals, and **landforms.** Landforms are physical features on the surface of Earth. **Geography** is the study of the relationship between physical features, climate, and people. At the end of the Stone Age, there were several **diverse,** or different, groups of people living in the Americas. Each group had its own culture. Each culture depended on resources available to it. Cultures used the plants, animals, and landforms in their areas. Cultures living in the desert used desert plants to make goods, such as baskets. Cultures living near mountains often used rocks to make tools and weapons. Fishing developed in cultures living near lakes or oceans. Villages began to form after people learned how to grow crops. During the Ice Age, a group of hunter-gatherers in Asia seemed to have developed boating skills. They might have migrated to islands in the Pacific. These people may have sailed to and contacted peoples living in the Americas.

Cultures Develop

Europe had many kinds of landforms, climates, and soil. As a result, many different complex cultures formed in Europe. Villages began to form after people learned better ways to farm. Cultures began using more of the resources that were available to them. Some crops, such as grains, lentils, and beans, grew all over Europe. Other crops needed a certain climate. Citrus fruits were grown in warmer climates. Apples were grown in mild climates. In the last 200 years, archaeologists found prehistoric paintings and drawings from these cultures. These artifacts give details about early people and their daily lives.

Prehistoric Art

Prehistoric cave paintings tell us the most about prehistoric cultures. Paintings of humans and animals were found at sites in Europe, Australia, and South Africa. Important cave paintings were found in Lascaux, France. These cave paintings are about 17,000 years old. Archaeologists discovered that the artists used their fingers or simple brushes to paint. Their paints were ground from nearby stones and mixed with animal fat or saliva. The paintings show that the people lived with and hunted horses, mammoth, and deer.

Lesson 3: Review

1. **Main Idea and Details** Fill in the missing details.

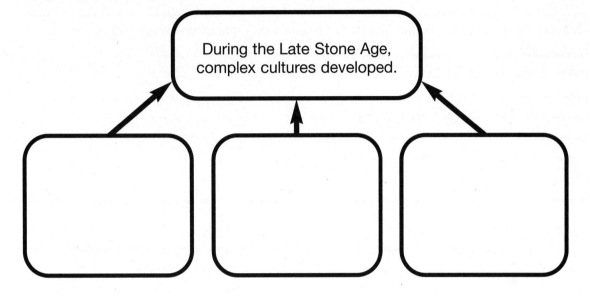

2. What is culture?

_____

_____

_____

3. What encouraged the development of culture in the Americas?

_____

_____

_____

4. What artifacts tell us the most about prehistoric cultures?

_____

_____

_____

5. **Critical Thinking:** *Make Inferences* How did landforms and climate influence cultures? Use the word **geography** in your answer.

_____

_____

_____

© Scott Foresman 6

Lesson 1: The Fertile Crescent

Vocabulary

civilization a group of people who live in a complex, organized society within a culture

fertile rich

plain a flat area of land

plateau an area of high, flat land

irrigation a system for watering crops

city-state a city with its own form of government, villages, and traditions

region an area of land with common physical features

artisan a craftsperson

Where Civilization Began

The earliest **civilizations** developed in southwestern Asia in about 3500 B.C. A civilization is a group of people who live in a complex, organized society within a culture. Civilizations developed in a part of southwest Asia that stretched from the eastern shores of the Mediterranean Sea to the Persian Gulf. We call this area the Fertile Crescent because its land was very **fertile,** or rich, and shaped like a crescent, or curve. A flat area of land, or **plain,** stretched between the Tigris and Euphrates Rivers. This plain became known as Mesopotamia, or "the land between the rivers." One of the first civilizations appeared in Mesopotamia.

Climate and Rivers

The climate in parts of the Fertile Crescent was not good for farming. It was very hot and dry in the summer. It either rained too much or not enough. In about 5000 B.C., farmers began to look for better land and climate. They moved from a **plateau,** or area of high, flat land, in the northern part of the Fertile Crescent. They settled on the plain between the Tigris and Euphrates Rivers. The rivers gave them a permanent source of water for farming. During seasons of low rainfall, farmers used the rivers to set up **irrigation** systems. Farmers dug trenches and ditches that brought water from the rivers to their fields.

The People

The people of southern Mesopotamia solved many problems. Mesopotamia did not have many resources. Yet the lack of trees and stones did not keep the people from building homes. They built huts out of reeds. Later they made bricks by mixing mud with straw. They used the bricks to build homes, temples, and palaces. They became expert farmers and developed better tools. They used the rivers to move goods. They were able to produce a surplus of food. The production of surplus food was a major step toward the rise of civilization in southern Mesopotamia.

Growth of City-States and Trade

The population in southern Mesopotamia grew as people became better farmers. New settlers arrived from different **regions** of the Fertile Crescent. By 3500 B.C., several villages became **city-states.** A city-state is a city that has become an independent state. A city-state has its own form of government, villages, and traditions. There was plenty of surplus food. People were able to work in other jobs besides farming. Some were **artisans,** or craftspeople, such as potters and weavers. Others were religious leaders, politicians, soldiers, or traders. Traders went on long journeys to trade with faraway peoples. They brought back goods that Mesopotamia lacked. Trade helped Mesopotamian culture spread to other parts of the world.

© Scott Foresman 6

Lesson 1: Review

1. **Cause and Effect** Fill in the missing effects.

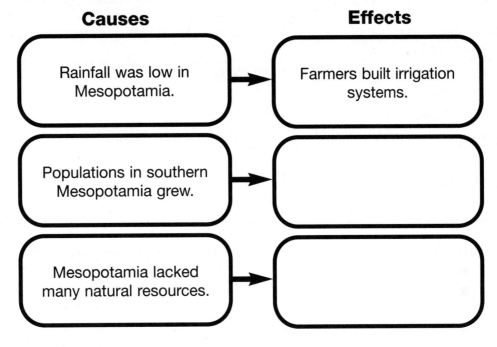

Causes   **Effects**

Rainfall was low in Mesopotamia. → Farmers built irrigation systems.

Populations in southern Mesopotamia grew. →

Mesopotamia lacked many natural resources. →

2. Where did the first civilizations arise?

_____

_____

3. How did Mesopotamian farmers use the Tigris and Euphrates Rivers to solve the problem of low rainfall?

_____

_____

4. What was one of the major steps toward the rise of civilization in southern Mesopotamia?

_____

_____

5. **Critical Thinking:** *Make Inferences* Why do you think settlers from other parts of the Fertile Crescent came to southern Mesopotamia?

_____

_____

© Scott Foresman 6

Lesson 2: Mesopotamia

Vocabulary

ziggurat a temple made up of a series of stacked rectangular platforms that form a pyramid-shaped structure

society an organized community with established rules and traditions

polytheism the worship of many gods

scribe a professional writer

cuneiform a form of wedge-shaped writing developed by the Sumerians

conquer to defeat and take over

empire a large territory that is controlled by one ruler

dynasty a ruling family

Sumer and Akkad

Early Mesopotamia was made up of the city-states of Sumer and Akkad. Sumer was in the south. Akkad was in the north. The Sumerians and Akkadians had similar customs, businesses, and religions. They spoke different languages. In about 3500 B.C., Sumer became more powerful than Akkad. Sumerian city-states built temple structures called **ziggurats.** A ziggurat was made up of a series of stacked rectangular platforms that formed a huge pyramid-shaped structure. Mesopotamians believed that ziggurats linked the heavens and Earth.

Religion and Government

Religion was an important part of Mesopotamian **society.** People in both Sumer and Akkad practiced **polytheism.** They worshipped many gods. The Sumerians believed that kings were chosen by the gods to carry out the gods' wishes. They also believed that kings passed the right to rule to their sons. These ideas about kingship would have an effect on later civilizations. Sumerian society was divided into classes. Wealthy people were at the top of the class system. Slaves were at the bottom. This kind of class system also affected later civilizations.

Writing

In about 3200 B.C., the Sumerians invented a system of writing. First they drew simple pictures that stood for objects or actions. Later this picture writing was made even simpler. A professional writer, or **scribe,** pressed a reed into wet clay to form wedge-shaped markings. These marks stood for objects, activities, or sounds. This new form of writing was called **cuneiform.** People used writing to keep records, tell stories, write letters, and set down laws.

The Rise and Fall of the Akkadian Empire

Sargon was an Akkadian ruler. He and his army **conquered,** or defeated, Sumer's city-states in about 2334 B.C. All of Mesopotamia came under Sargon's rule. This formed the world's first **empire.** An empire is a large territory of many different places controlled by one ruler. The Akkadian **dynasty,** or ruling family, was in power for about 150 years. By 2100 B.C., the Sumerian city-state of Ur rose to power.

Sumer's Final Days

Between 2100 B.C. and 2000 B.C., the city-state of Ur in Sumer controlled Mesopotamia. Farming, business, and culture thrived. The oldest known written law code was created at this time. Many important structures, such as the Ziggurat of Ur, were built during this period. The Ziggurat of Ur is thought to be one of the largest ziggurats ever built. In about 2000 B.C., Sumer lost power. The contributions of the Sumerians helped other civilizations to rise. These contributions include cuneiform, ziggurats, and the wheel.

© Scott Foresman 6

Lesson 2: Review

1. **Main Idea and Details** Fill in the missing main idea and detail below.

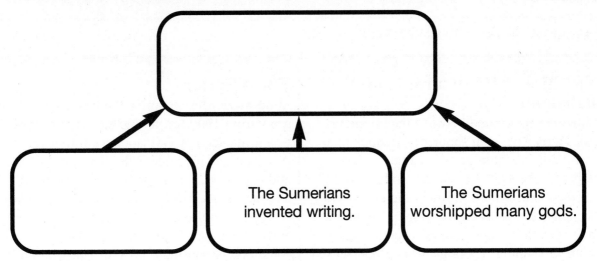

The Sumerians invented writing.

The Sumerians worshipped many gods.

2. How were Sumerian religion and government connected?

_____

_____

3. How did the Sumerian writing system develop and change? Use the word **cuneiform** in your answer.

_____

_____

4. Describe an example of an idea or invention that shaped Mesopotamian civilization and influenced other civilizations.

_____

_____

5. **Critical Thinking:** *Recognize Point of View* After Sumer rose again, does it seem that the Mesopotamians continued to make important advances? Explain.

_____

_____

Lesson 3: Babylonia and Assyria

Vocabulary

conquest the defeat of another group

The Rise of Hammurabi and Babylonia

Babylon was located between the Euphrates and Tigris Rivers, in southern Mesopotamia. In 1792 B.C., Hammurabi became king of Babylon. By 1754 B.C., he controlled all of Mesopotamia and its surrounding city-states. His empire was called Babylonia. Hammurabi taxed people's properties. He used the tax money to support his large army. He also used the tax money to pay for many new construction projects. He was considered a shrewd, or clever, ruler.

Babylonian Civilization

Life under Hammurabi did not change much. People still irrigated their crops. They still traded. Babylon became a center of culture and learning. There were advances in mathematics, literature, and law. Hammurabi established a set of laws that helped him rule his empire. The Code of Hammurabi contained 282 laws. This set of laws protected weak people. Hammurabi's code also called for punishments that fit the crime.

The Assyrians

In northern Mesopotamia, the Assyrian culture grew from 1900 B.C. to 600 B.C. This culture was influenced by Babylonian culture. Yet Assyrian culture placed a higher value on wars and **conquest.** Conquest is the defeat of another group. From 688 B.C. to 627 B.C., the Assyrian Empire controlled almost all of the Fertile Crescent. It was ruled by King Ashurbanipal during this time. The king built a great library at Nineveh.

Babylonia Grows

In 605 B.C., Nebuchadnezzar II became king of Babylon. He took over much of the former Assyrian Empire. He started projects to make Babylon powerful again. He built many temples and buildings. Babylon was once again an important center of learning. Babylonians made important discoveries in mathematics. Babylonian astronomers were able to correctly judge when the eclipses of the moon and the sun would occur. The Babylonian Empire was taken over by the Persians in 539 B.C.

Lesson 3: Review

1. ↻ **Sequence** The following events are not in the correct order. List them in the correct order.

_____ Nebuchadnezzar II starts a series of building projects in Babylon.

_____ Hammurabi establishes his code of law.

_____ Ashurbanipal builds his library at Nineveh.

2. Who was Hammurabi?

_____

_____

_____

3. What was the Code of Hammurabi?

_____

_____

_____

4. How did Assyrian culture differ from Babylonian culture? Use the word **conquest** in your answer.

_____

_____

_____

5. **Critical Thinking:** *Make Generalizations* What contributions did the Babylonians make to civilization?

_____

_____

_____

Lesson 4: Hebrews, Phoenicians, and Lydians

Vocabulary

covenant an agreement

monotheism the worship of one God

slavery the practice of one person owning another

descendant a person who is born later into the same family

barter to exchange one kind of goods and services for another

The Hebrews

Abraham is considered to be the founder of Judaism. The Hebrew Bible says that God spoke to Abraham and told him to leave his homeland and go to a land called Canaan. According to the Hebrew Bible, God and Abraham made an agreement, or **covenant,** in about 1800 B.C. Abraham promised to worship only one God. In exchange, God promised to look after Abraham and his people—later known as the Hebrews. **Monotheism** is the worship of one God. Judaism was one of the first monotheistic religions. Later the Hebrews moved from Canaan to Egypt. The Egyptians forced them into **slavery.** Slavery is the practice of one person owning another person. According to the Hebrew Bible, God chose Moses to lead the Hebrews to freedom. The Hebrew Bible also states that God gave Moses the Ten Commandments. The Ten Commandments guided people in how to worship. It also set down rules to help people live good lives. All of Abraham's **descendants,** as well as people who were escaping from Egypt, were to follow the Ten Commandments.

The Hebrew Bible

The Torah contains the first five books of the Hebrew Bible. These books provide guidance and laws for the Jewish people. They also contain historical information and stories important to Judaism.

Israel and Judah

The Hebrews in Canaan lived in about 12 different tribes. The tribes defeated the Canaanites sometime between 1200 B.C. and 1125 B.C. In about 1000 B.C., King David united the Hebrew tribes. He founded a kingdom called Israel. Its capital was Jerusalem. David's son, Solomon, built a temple in Jerusalem to house the Torah and to be a place of worship. After Solomon's death, the kingdom split into two. Israel was in the north. Judah was in the south.

Judaism Today

Today, millions of people practice Judaism. Jewish people still read the Torah. They celebrate Jewish holidays such as Passover. Passover honors the escape of the Hebrews from Egypt. Rabbis teach Jews how to read the Torah. In Hebrew, *rabbi* means "master" or "teacher."

Phoenicians and Lydians

The Phoenicians lived along the eastern edge of the Mediterranean Sea during the time of King Solomon. They were great sailors and traders. Through trade, they linked various parts of the ancient world. New ideas as well as goods were exchanged through trade. The Phoenicians helped develop the modern alphabet. People during this time usually **bartered,** or exchanged one kind of goods and services for another. The Lydians invented the region's first coins by 500 B.C. Coins made trading simpler and easier.

© Scott Foresman 6

Lesson 4: Review

1. **Main Idea and Details** Fill in the main idea below.

```
                    ┌─────────────────────┐
                    │                     │
                    │                     │
                    └─────────────────────┘
          ↗                  ↑                  ↖
┌──────────────────┐ ┌──────────────────┐ ┌──────────────────┐
│ King David united │ │  The tribes of    │ │ In about 1000 B.C.,│
│   the tribes of   │ │     Israel        │ │ King David founded │
│     Israel.       │ │ defeated the      │ │ the kingdom of     │
│                   │ │  Canaanites.      │ │     Israel.        │
└──────────────────┘ └──────────────────┘ └──────────────────┘
```

2. What was one of the first monotheistic religions?

   _____

   _____

3. What was the purpose of Solomon's temple?

   _____

   _____

4. What did the Lydians invent that we use today?

   _____

   _____

5. **Critical Thinking:** *Make Generalizations* How did the Phoenicians help spread new ideas from one part of the ancient world to another?

   _____

   _____

Lesson 1: The Lifeline of the Nile

Vocabulary

delta a triangular-shaped area of soil at the mouth of a river

silt a mixture of soil and small rocks

papyrus a plant that was used to make paper

cataract a waterfall

The Nile River Valley

The Nile River has provided water for civilizations in northeastern Africa for thousands of years. The Nile River is surrounded by deserts. It is more than 4,000 miles long and is the longest river in the world. The river begins in East Africa and flows northward into Egypt. Egypt is a country in the Nile River Valley. The Nile flows through a **delta,** a triangular-shaped area of soil at the mouth of a river. A delta looks like fingers spread out. Water flowing northward carried **silt,** a mixture of soil and small rocks. The river brought silt to the delta. Egyptian civilization began along the Nile River. The Nile irrigated land that stretched about 5 miles on both sides of the Nile.

Giver of Life

The Nile River overflowed every year because of heavy rains. People living along the river planted seeds in the fertile soil after the flood waters went down. They harvested crops in late summer. Much of the land near the Nile was desert. Without the river, crops could not be grown. People would not have enough water to survive. Ancient Egyptians grew a crop called **papyrus.** They made paper from this plant. The Nile was used to move goods. But travelers had to watch out for the Nile's six **cataracts,** or waterfalls. They made it impossible to sail directly from the Nile Delta south to East Africa without taking a boat out of water and carrying it. The Nile gave the Egyptians many gifts to help their civilization develop.

Taker of Life

The Nile flooded at about the same time each year. But this flooding was not always the same. Sometimes it flooded too much and destroyed crops and killed people. Other times, the river did not flood enough. Crops would not grow. When crops failed, the Egyptians used crops they kept from earlier harvests. The Egyptians built irrigation canals to bring water to their crops. The Egyptians wanted to find out why the Nile flooded differently each year. The Egyptians watched sunrises, sunsets, and how the moon looked every evening. They used this information to figure out when the Nile might flood. They made a calendar to keep track of the number of days between floods. This calendar helped them determine that the Nile flooded between May and September. The irrigation canals and calendar helped solve their problems with the Nile.

Lesson 1: Review

1. ↻ **Summarize** Fill in the missing detail below.

| | Sometimes the Nile flooded too much or not enough. | The Egyptians made calendars to keep track of when the Nile would flood. |

Even though the Nile flooded, it was important to the Egyptians.

2. Describe the route of the Nile River. Use the word **delta** in your answer.

_____

_____

_____

3. What solutions did the Egyptians come up with to deal with the flooding of the Nile?

_____

_____

_____

4. How was the Nile a giver and taker of life?

_____

_____

_____

5. Critical Thinking: *Make Inferences* Suppose the Egyptians had not tried to predict when the Nile would flood. Do you think their civilization would have lasted very long? Explain your answer.

_____

_____

_____

Lesson 2: Life in Egypt

Vocabulary

> **unify** to join together
>
> **pharaoh** a god-king
>
> **hieroglyphics** a form of writing made up of pictures and symbols
>
> **pyramid** a large stone building that served as a house or tomb for the dead
>
> **mummy** a preserved body
>
> **economy** the way people use and manage resources

Unifying Egypt

Upper Egypt and Lower Egypt were **unified,** or joined together, into one country. Legend says that King Menes led his army into Lower Egypt and joined the two kingdoms in about 3150 B.C. Historians divided ancient Egypt into the Old Kingdom (c. 2575–2181 B.C.), the Middle Kingdom (c. 2040–1782 B.C.), and the New Kingdom (c. 1570–1070 B.C.). During the New Kingdom, the king became known as the **pharaoh,** or god-king.

Egyptian Records

Like the Sumerians, the Egyptians developed a type of writing based on pictures. This writing is called **hieroglyphics,** or "sacred carvings." The pictures stood for objects and ideas. Unlike Sumerian cuneiform, the Egyptian pictures also stood for sounds. A passage on the Rosetta Stone was written in Greek and Egyptian. Archaeologists read Egyptian hieroglyphics by comparing them to the Greek words. Priests, officials, and scribes, or professional writers, kept written records. These records help archaeologists understand ancient Egyptian life.

Pyramid Building

Old Kingdom pharaohs built **pyramids,** or large stone tombs for dead pharaohs. Egyptians believed that pharaohs were gods even after they died. Pyramids were filled with all the pharaoh's possessions. The pharaoh's preserved body, or **mummy,** was placed in the pyramid.

Social Life

Trade grew during the Middle Kingdom. A new middle class came into being. In the new class system, the pharaoh was at the top. Then came nobles and priests. Next were merchants, craftspeople, and scribes. Then came farmers and unskilled workers. Enslaved people were at the bottom of the class system. Egyptians could move between classes. Like Sumerian women, Egyptian women could inherit land and take part in business. Most women were not taught to read and write.

Trade and Technology

During the Middle Kingdom, the Egyptian **economy** became stronger. An economy is the way people use and manage resources. The Hyksos from Asia took over Egypt in about 1660 B.C. After about 100 years, the Egyptian pharaohs took over again. This began the New Kingdom.

New Kingdom Pharaohs

Middle Kingdom and New Kingdom pharaohs ruled with their sons or wives. In 1350 B.C., Amenhotep IV became pharaoh. He and his wife Nefertiti began to worship a new sun god called Aton. Amenhotep neglected his duties as pharaoh. The next pharaoh, Tutankhamen, brought back order to Egypt. Aton was no longer worshipped.

© Scott Foresman 6

Lesson 2: Review

1. ⟳ **Summarize** Fill in the missing detail in the blank box below.

```
┌─────────────────┐   ┌─────────────────┐   ┌─────────────────┐
│  Pharaohs were  │   │ The Egyptians   │   │                 │
│ considered      │   │ built pyramids  │   │                 │
│ god-kings.      │   │ for the         │   │                 │
│                 │   │ pharaohs.       │   │                 │
└─────────────────┘   └─────────────────┘   └─────────────────┘
          │                    │                     │
          ▼                    ▼                     ▼
            ┌──────────────────────────────────┐
            │  Pharaohs were very important     │
            │       to the Egyptians.           │
            └──────────────────────────────────┘
```

2. According to legend, how was Egypt unified?

_____

_____

_____

3. What are hieroglyphics and how do we know what they mean?

_____

_____

_____

4. How was Egyptian culture similar to and different from Sumerian culture?

_____

_____

_____

5. **Critical Thinking:** *Evaluate Information* Why was trade important to the Egyptians? Use the word **economy** in your answer.

_____

_____

_____

Lesson 3: Nubia and Egypt

Vocabulary

independent free

Lands South of Egypt

Nubia was a kingdom south of Egypt. Part of Nubia now makes up the African country of Sudan. Archaeologists believe people have been living in Nubia since about 3200 B.C. Unlike in Egypt, tall cliffs of granite rock surrounded parts of the Nile in Nubia. The soil in Nubia was rockier than in Egypt. Like the Egyptians, the Nubians built irrigation canals to get water from the Nile to their crops. The written Nubian language was called Meroitic. It was much like Egyptian hieroglyphics. People today are still unable to read Meroitic. Most of what we know about Nubia comes from Egyptian writings. Both the Nubians and the Egyptians believed in many gods. The Nubians may have also worshipped Egyptian gods. Nubians believed in an afterlife and built pyramids. Nubian pyramids were smaller and shaped differently than Egyptian pyramids.

Interaction

By about 2575 B.C., the Egyptians invaded Nubia. They were looking for resources. Egypt depended on Nubia for trade goods such as gold, ivory, cattle, and granite. Egypt set up trading centers and forts to protect its trade routes in Nubia. In the 1800s B.C., Egypt took over land in northern Nubia. This land included Kush, a Nubian kingdom. In about 1650 B.C., during the Hyksos rule of Egypt, Kush became **independent,** or free. In the 1400s B.C., Egypt took over Nubia again. At the end of the New Kingdom, Egypt became weak and Kush again became independent. Kush began to take over all of Egypt by about 750 B.C. The Kushite kings then became pharaohs of Egypt.

Kush Rises

Many groups tried to take Egypt from the Kushite kings. In about 670 B.C., the Assyrians attacked Egypt. The Kushites moved south to their capital at Napata. After 600 B.C., the Egyptians regained power and destroyed Napata. The Kushites founded a new capital at Meroë and trade grew. Meroë was rich in iron. Traders from other lands wanted tools and weapons made out of iron. Egyptians used bronze tools when they built pyramids. Women in Kush became queens as they did in Egypt. Egypt grew weaker and influenced Kush less. Meroë remained a great trade center until A.D. 350.

Lesson 3 Review

1. ⟳ **Summarize** Fill in the missing detail in the blank box.

The Egyptians and Nubians shared some aspects of culture.		The Egyptians invaded Nubia and set up trade and military posts to protect resources.

The Nubians and Egyptians interacted.

2. How was the geography of Nubia different from Egypt?

_____

_____

_____

3. Why did the ancient Egyptians and Nubians interact?

_____

_____

_____

4. Why did other groups of people want to conquer Egypt? What impact did this have on Nubia?

_____

_____

_____

5. **Critical Thinking:** *Make Inferences* Why do you think that the peaceful relationship between the Egyptians and Nubians changed over time?

_____

_____

_____

Lesson 1: The Geography of China

Vocabulary

loess a yellowish-brown soil that blows in from the desert

terrace a platform of earth that looks like a stair

levee a wide wall that is built next to a river to keep it from flooding

double cropping a way of farming in which two crops are grown on the same land in the same year

A Land of Differences

Civilizations grew up in China about 3000 B.C. Today China is the largest country in Asia. It is the third largest country in the world. More people live in China than in any other country. Different parts of China have different landforms, climates, and ways of life.

The North China Plain

Historians believe human settlement and culture in China began on the North China Plain. The North China Plain is in eastern China. Many people now live there. It is a center of agriculture and industry. Much of China's food is produced there. Land on the plain has **loess,** or yellowish-brown soil that blows in from the desert. Crops such as soybeans, wheat, and cotton are grown on **terraces,** or platforms of earth that look like stairs. Beijing, the capital of China, is on the plain. The city has been a center of culture and government for a long time.

China's Sorrow

The Huang He, or Huang River, flows through the North China Plain. Early civilizations in China grew in the Huang River Valley in about 3000 B.C. The river picks up and carries yellow silt that turns the water yellow. The river gets its name from this color. *Huang* means "yellow" in Chinese. On the North China Plain, the Huang slows down. Floods happen during heavy summer rains. **Levees** are wide walls that were built next to rivers to help control flooding. The Huang has been called "China's Sorrow" because its floods have destroyed crops and homes.

Guangxi Zhungzu

Guangxi Zhungzu is in southeastern China. It has a good climate for farming. Farmers use a type of farming called **double cropping.** Two crops are grown on the same land in the same year. Fishing is also important here. The area has sinkholes, caves, mountains, underground streams, and limestone hills.

To The Roof of the World

The Tibetan Plateau is a rocky area of China with mountain ranges. The people who live here are called the Zhuang. Many Zhuang are nomads, or people who travel from place to place. The climate and food are different in different parts of the plateau. The Tibetan Plateau is sometimes called the Roof of the World. The Himalayas, a mountain range that has the tallest peak on Earth, are on the Tibetan Plateau.

© Scott Foresman 6

Lesson 1: Review

1. ↻ **Summarize** Fill in the missing fact.

	The Huang River irrigates land on the North China Plain.	The Huang River is controlled by using levees.

The Huang, or "yellow," River irrigates land but must be controlled by using levees.

2. How has the Huang River affected people living near it? Use the word **levee** in your answer.

_____

_____

3. What gives the Huang River its name?

_____

_____

4. How does China's geography show differences within the large country?

_____

_____

5. **Critical Thinking:** *Make Inferences* Is it possible to make generalizations about the people of China based on where they live? Explain.

_____

_____

Lesson 2: China's Past

Vocabulary

pictograph a picture that stands for a word

oracle bone a shell or bone used during the Shang dynasty to tell the future

province a region of a country

ancestor a family member who lived before a grandparent did

civil service the practice of using skills and talents to work in the government

middleman a person who goes between buyers and sellers

Picturing Chinese History

Chinese culture is the oldest culture that exists today. Chinese writing, art, and archaeological remains show how much the Chinese culture has stayed the same. The Chinese language is written in **pictographs,** or pictures that stand for words. The written language has stayed similar for centuries.

Ancient Voices

Chinese people told legends about people and the world. The stories show the importance of animals, agriculture, and inventions. Many legends come from the Xia period, about 2000–1700 B.C.

The Shang Dynasty

The first Chinese dynasty was the Shang dynasty, which began between 1760 and 1500 B.C. Most people in the Huang River Valley were farmers. Bronze was used to make tools, cups, weapons, and goods. **Oracle bones** were used to tell the future. The Shang people kept the first written records in China.

The Longest Dynasty

The Zhou dynasty began in 1027 B.C. It lasted more than 800 years. The early part of the Zhou was called Western Zhou. Most people were farmers. Some had slaves. Silk cloth was important to the economy.

Eastern Zhou Dynasties

The second part of the Zhou dynasty, the Eastern Zhou, lasted from about 770 B.C. to 221 B.C. Trade and the economy did well. Projects included flood control, irrigation, and canal building. Iron was used to make tools and weapons.

The First Emperor

In 221 B.C., the king of the strongest state became Shi Huangdi, or the "first emperor," under the Qin dynasty. Qin was divided into 36 **provinces,** or states. The Great Wall of China was built to protect the empire from northern invaders. Builders connected defensive walls that had been built earlier. Systems of money and weights and measures were made the same in all regions. Shi Huangdi wanted to control what people talked about and studied. People wanted freedom and they fought against the emperor.

Han Dynasty

The Han dynasty lasted from 206 B.C. to A.D. 220. The first ruler, Han Gaozu, gave people more freedom. He allowed them to read any books they wanted. Han Gaozu's name means "High Ancestor." An **ancestor** is a relative who lived before a grandparent did. During the Han dynasty, roads were built. Trade goods were taxed. The first Chinese history book was written. **Civil service** was started. For the first time, anyone who passed a civil service test could work for the government. These advancements made China more unified.

Inventions

During the Han dynasty, porcelain, paper, and ink were invented. **Middlemen,** or people who go between buyers and sellers, traded these goods on the Silk Road.

Lesson 2: Review

1. 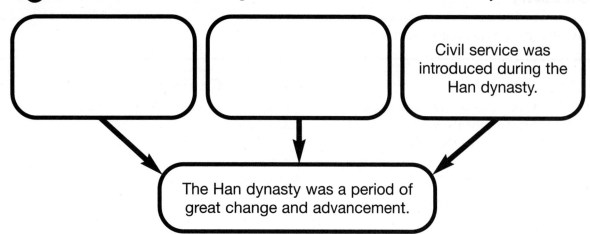 **Summarize** Fill in the blank spaces with two details from the summary below.

Civil service was introduced during the Han dynasty.

The Han dynasty was a period of great change and advancement.

2. Name some of the things that people may have done in their daily lives during the Zhou dynasty.

_____

_____

_____

3. How did Chinese culture become more unified during the Han dynasty?

_____

_____

_____

4. What inventions were made in China's early history?

_____

_____

_____

5. **Critical Thinking:** *Make Inferences* Why do you think that Shi Huangdi wanted to connect the defensive walls into what became the Great Wall of China?

_____

_____

_____

Lesson 3: Legacy of Thought

Vocabulary

nobility a high-ranking social class

Master Kung

In China, Confucius is known as Kung Fuzi, or Master Kung. Confucius was born in 551 B.C. His family was part of the **nobility,** a high-ranking social class. He became a scholar, or a very educated thinker and teacher. During his life, the Zhou dynasty was coming to an end. Many people were cruel and greedy. Confucius taught people the difference between right and wrong. He valued order and peace. He was an advisor at a king's court for many years. Many people went to him for advice. It is said that Master Kung had about 3,000 followers by the time of his death in 479 B.C.

The Master's Work

The *Analects* is a collection of sayings by Confucius. These sayings were written down by his students. In the *Analects,* Confucius gives advice on how to do the right thing. The teachings of Confucius are known as Confucianism. Confucianism teaches respect for all people. It also says that people should take the middle way, or make balanced decisions. Confucianism teaches that people should accept their positions in society. Confucius believed that people should treat others the way they would like to be treated. He also felt that children must obey, respect, and honor their parents and teachers. Confucianism taught respect for the ruler. He felt that a ruler had the Mandate of Heaven, or the right to govern for the good of all people. A good ruler brought times of richness and peace. Bad or unwise rulers could be pushed off the throne by the people.

Beyond Confucianism

During Confucius's life there were many other scholars. Because there were so many scholars, this time was called the "hundred schools of thought." Mencius was a follower of Confucius who taught that all people were good. Daoism is the belief in finding the "way," or the dao, of the universe. Daoists believed that people should live in harmony with nature. Confucianism and Daoism both greatly influenced Chinese culture.

© Scott Foresman 6

Lesson 3: Review

1. **Summarize** Fill in the missing detail in the blank below.

```
┌────────────────────┐  ┌────────────────────┐  ┌────────────────────┐
│ The teachings of   │  │                    │  │ The "hundred schools │
│ Confucius are      │  │                    │  │ of thought" influenced│
│ important to       │  │                    │  │ Chinese culture.    │
│ understanding      │  │                    │  │                     │
│ China's history.   │  │                    │  │                     │
└────────────────────┘  └────────────────────┘  └────────────────────┘
              ↘              ↓              ↙
        ┌──────────────────────────────────────┐
        │  Confucianism, Daoism, and the         │
        │  "hundred schools of thought"          │
        │  influenced Chinese culture            │
        │  and history.                          │
        └──────────────────────────────────────┘
```

2. Briefly explain three Confucian principles.

   _____

   _____

3. What is the *Analects?*

   _____

   _____

4. Besides Confucianism, what other way of thinking has had much influence in China?

   _____

   _____

5. **Critical Thinking:** *Make Generalizations* How have Confucianism and Daoism influenced Chinese culture?

   _____

   _____

Lesson 1: Geography of South Asia

Vocabulary

subcontinent a large region separated by water from other land areas

monsoon season the rainy season

subsistence farming a type of farming in which people grow food just for their family's use

A Diamond Breaks Away

South Asia is a diamond-shaped land that extends far into the Indian Ocean. The world's tallest mountains, the Himalayas, are in South Asia. South Asia is called a **subcontinent** because it is very large and separated by water from other land areas. Scientists believe that Earth's surface is made of several slowly moving plates. The subcontinent may have once been part of a huge landmass. But its plate broke away and pushed into a larger plate. The smaller plate pushing up under the larger plate formed the Himalayas. The highest peak of the Himalayas is Mount Everest.

Snow to Monsoon

Eight countries are part of South Asia—Pakistan, Nepal, Bhutan, Afghanistan, Bangladesh, India, Sri Lanka, and the Maldives Islands or Maldives. Pakistan is in the northwestern part of South Asia. It has the world's second tallest mountain, called the K2. A desert stretches across part of Pakistan and northwestern India. Nepal and Bhutan are mountainous countries in the east and north. To the south, a river delta surrounds Bangladesh. India is farther south. It has the Himalayas, a plain, and a plateau. Sri Lanka and the Maldives are islands in the Indian Ocean. Temperatures in South Asia are cool from October through February. It is very hot from March through May. The **monsoon season,** or rainy season, lasts from June through September. Nearly all of the yearly precipitation, or rain and snow, falls during the monsoon season.

Great Rivers, Great Plain

The Indus, the Ganges, and the Brahmaputra Rivers flow through South Asia. The rivers begin in the Himalayas and flow over the Indo-Gangetic Plain, or the Indo-Ganges Plain. The rivers carry water and silt to farmlands to irrigate crops and make the soil rich. The monsoon season rains cause flooding, which spreads the silt more. Families either grow food for themselves or trade with small groups of people in their villages. This type of farming is known as **subsistence farming.**

Plateau, Coast, and Islands

The Deccan Plateau is south of the Indo-Ganges Plain. The climate is dry. The soil is rich. Cotton and peanuts are grown there. The Western Ghats and the Eastern Ghats are mountains that border the Deccan plateau. Most people in India work as farmers. People also fish. Sri Lanka and the Maldives Islands export tea, coconuts, fish, and rubber. Manufacturing, clothing, and textiles are also important industries.

© Scott Foresman 6

Lesson 1: Review

1. ↻ **Summarize** Fill in the missing detail below.

```
┌─────────────────────┐   ┌─────────────────────┐   ┌─────────────────────┐
│ Mount Everest rises │   │ The Indo-Ganges Plain│   │                     │
│ in South Asia.      │   │ provides good farmland│  │                     │
│                     │   │ in South Asia.       │   │                     │
└─────────────────────┘   └─────────────────────┘   └─────────────────────┘
            ↘                      ↓                      ↙
              ┌──────────────────────────────────────┐
              │ South Asia has various physical        │
              │ features and landforms.                │
              └──────────────────────────────────────┘
```

2. Why is South Asia called a subcontinent?

_____

_____

_____

3. How do many people farm on the Indo-Ganges Plain?

_____

_____

_____

4. What does the geography of South Asia reveal about the many differences within the subcontinent?

_____

_____

_____

5. **Critical Thinking: *Make Generalizations*** What generalizations can you make about the ways of life of South Asian peoples by looking at pictures showing their environments, homes, and work? Look at the pictures included in Lesson 1 of your textbook.

_____

_____

_____

Lesson 2: India and Persia

Vocabulary

brahmin a priest or a teacher; the highest position in Aryan society

sudra a serf; the lowest position in Aryan society

Indus River Valley Civilization

Civilization in the Indus River Valley began about 2500 B.C. Two ancient cities were Harappa and Mohenjo-Daro. The people had a system of writing. People farmed and stored grain, worked with metal and pottery, wove cotton, and traded and sold goods. By 2500 B.C., the Harappan civilization was strong. In Mohenjo-Daro, the people constructed buildings and roads. About 1700 B.C., the Harappan civilization vanished suddenly. Many archaeologists think that this was because of a monsoon, a flood, or an earthquake.

The Aryans Arrive

About 1500 B.C., the Aryans invaded the Indus River Valley. They came over the Hindu Kush mountains in the north. This is called the Aryan migration. The Aryans spoke a language called Sanskrit. They were nomads who herded cattle, sheep, and goats. The Aryans built villages and towns where they farmed and traded. The Vedas, or "Books of Knowledge," contain their stories, songs, and history. The Vedas describe wars between groups of Aryans as well as contests between gods and humans. The Aryans also wrote hymns.

Aryan Culture Spreads

Aryan groups were led by a rajah, or priest leader. The groups traded with each other. They fought one another. The highest positions in Aryan society were held by priests and teachers, or **brahmins.** Warriors and kings were the second highest group. Artisans, traders, and merchants were in the third group. The **sudras,** or the serfs who farmed and served others, were at the lowest level. The Persians heard about Aryan riches. Persian armies moved into the Indus River Valley.

The Persian Empire

From about 550 to 320 B.C., the Persian Empire reached from the Mediterranean Sea to the Indus River Valley. King Darius I made India part of the Persian Empire. The Persians built roads to India and developed trade. This connected India to lands in Central Asia. Zoroastrianism is a religion founded by the Persian prophet Zoroaster. Zoroastrianism recognized one god. Today's followers of Zoroastrianism are known as Parsis. Many live in South Asia today. Their ancestors came from Persia.

The First Indian Empire

Chandragupta Maurya took over India in about 320 B.C. He began the first Indian Empire, the Mauryan Empire. He extended the empire to the Persian border. Ashoka, Chandragupta's grandson, became the ruler of India in about 270 B.C. By that time, the Mauryan Empire included the Deccan Plateau. Ashoka organized the empire's government. It controlled many parts of life, such as how artisans worked and how doctors treated their patients. India had a strong group of civil service workers, a powerful army, and even had spies to watch over the empire. The Mauryan Empire ended about 185 B.C. India broke up into regions until A.D. 320, when the Guptas took over.

Arts and Sciences

The Gupta Empire lasted about 200 years. Achievements were made in astronomy, mathematics, literature, poetry, art, and architecture. Economy and trade improved. The Huns, people from the north, arrived in the fifth century. They took control of much of India by the mid-sixth century.

© Scott Foresman 6

Lesson 2: Review

1. ⟳ **Summarize** Fill in the missing detail that completes the summary.

Chandragupta Maurya extended the empire to the Persian border.

Ashoka organized the government of the Mauryan Empire.

The Mauryan Empire expanded and became organized under Chandragupta Maurya and Ashoka.

2. What was the Aryan migration?

_____

_____

3. How did the Persian Empire influence Indian civilization and culture?

_____

_____

4. What are the most important stages in the development of Indian culture from 2500 B.C. to A.D. 300?

_____

_____

5. **Critical Thinking:** *Evaluate Information* How do the Vedas, poems, and epics of the Aryan people reflect their culture?

_____

_____

© Scott Foresman 6

Lesson 3: Hinduism

Vocabulary

reincarnation the process in which a person goes from one life to the next life

caste a lifelong social group into which a person is born

Seeds of Belief

The main religion in India is Hinduism. It is one of the world's oldest religions. Hinduism does not have a founder. Hinduism probably started with the religious beliefs of the Aryans and the first people of the Indus River Valley. There are four Vedas in Hinduism. The oldest is the Rig Veda. It contains more than 1,000 hymns that are dedicated to Aryan gods. Hindus recite verses from the Vedas. Today Hindus still sing hymns from the Rig Veda at ceremonies such as weddings and funerals. However, some of the beliefs and practices of Hindus have changed over time.

Gods and Goddesses

Hindus believe in many gods and goddesses. They also have many different beliefs. Some Hindus believe in only one universal being, Brahman. Three of the main forms of Brahman are the gods Brahma (the creator), Vishnu (the preserver), and Shiva (the destroyer). Hindus believe that Vishnu controls dharma, which is the order of the universe. Other Hindu gods and goddesses are forms of Brahman.

Seven Truths and Reincarnation

Seven doctrines, or truths, are important Hindu beliefs. These doctrines include peaceful living, freedom of thought, respect for nature and animals, becoming one with Brahman, and that good and bad actions will one day affect us. Hindus believe that after a person dies, he or she is reborn into a new life. The process of going from one life into the next is called **reincarnation.** If Hindus live good lives, then their karma is good. Karma means the lifetime actions of a person. With good karma, a Hindu's rebirth is good. The goal of a Hindu is to end rebirth and become one with Brahman.

Way of Life

Hindus in India traditionally belong to a **caste.** A caste is a lifelong social group into which a person is born. This tradition dates back to the time of the Vedas. During this time, jobs and marriage depended upon a person's caste. Priests and teachers were in the highest caste. Rulers and warriors were in the next caste. The lowest castes were servants of all others. The lowest caste members were given the jobs that no one else was willing to do. These people were called "untouchables." The caste system is still part of life in India. There are laws against mistreating members of other castes.

© Scott Foresman 6

Lesson 3: Review

1. **Summarize** Fill in the missing detail about Hindu beliefs below.

Hindus recite verses from the Vedas.		Hindus believe in reincarnation.

The Vedas, Hindu gods and goddesses, and reincarnation are important to followers of Hinduism.

2. What are Hinduism's roots?

_____

_____

3. What are the three main forms of Brahman, the universal truth?

_____

_____

4. What are the main points of Hindu beliefs?

_____

_____

5. **Critical Thinking:** *Fact or Opinion* Is the following statement a fact or an opinion? The caste system is still part of daily life in India.

_____

_____

Lesson 4: Buddhism

Vocabulary

meditation a way of clearing the mind
enlightenment a state of pure goodness

Who Was the Buddha?

The sixth century B.C. was a time when Asian people were fighting and questioning religion. Buddhist tradition says that Siddhartha Gautama was the man who became known as the Buddha. The Buddha founded the religion of Buddhism. Siddhartha was born just south of the Himalayas in about 563 B.C. His father was a wealthy ruler. His father was told that Siddhartha would be a great king if he stayed at home. He would become a great teacher if he left home. When Siddhartha was a child, his father kept him within the palace walls. As an adult, Siddhartha left the palace and began his travels.

The Buddha's Travels

Siddhartha joined a group of monks. They fasted, or lived on very little food, for six years. The monks believed that by giving up what the body needs, they might better understand what the spirit needs. They practiced **meditation,** a way of clearing the mind. Siddhartha left the group. According to Buddhist tradition, Siddhartha sat silently under a tree near Bodh Gaya and meditated. When he saw a beautiful morning star, he realized that all people had the power to free themselves from suffering. He believed that he reached **enlightenment,** or a state of pure goodness. He became known as the Buddha. For nearly 50 years, he traveled and taught. His followers believe that he spoke to all people using a language that everyone could understand. The Buddha taught that people, not just priests, could achieve enlightenment. His words showed a peaceful and tolerant way of looking at the world.

Four and Eight

Buddhism is based on the Four Noble Truths. The Four Noble Truths explain human suffering. The Buddha used these truths to understand his enlightenment.

The Four Noble Truths are listed below:

1. Suffering is part of life for all people.
2. People suffer because they want so many things in life.
3. If people can free themselves from wanting so many things, they will not suffer.
4. People can free themselves from wants and from suffering by following the Eightfold Path.

The Eightfold Path is a way of living that can help people find relief from their suffering. According to the Eightfold Path, people should develop three qualities: wisdom, morality, and meditation. The Eightfold Path suggests actions, efforts, or ways of thinking that will help Buddhists develop these qualities.

© Scott Foresman 6

Lesson 4: Review

1. **Summarize** Fill in the blank with a main belief of Buddhism.

Buddhism is based on the Four Noble Truths.		Buddhists follow the teachings of the Buddha.

The Four Noble Truths, the Eightfold Path, and the teachings of the Buddha are important to Buddhists.

2. According to Buddhist tradition, who was the Buddha?

_____

_____

3. How are the Four Noble Truths and the Eightfold Path connected in Buddhism?

_____

_____

4. Why could Buddhism be considered a peaceful philosophy and why might it appeal to people?

_____

_____

5. **Critical Thinking:** *Make Generalizations* How do the ideas of Buddhism attempt to solve some of life's difficult problems? Use the words **meditation** and **enlightenment** in your answer.

_____

_____

Lesson 1: Geography of Mesoamerica

Vocabulary

peninsula an arm of land sticking into the sea so that it is nearly surrounded by water

cenote a natural well

A Land of Rugged Mountains

Mesoamerica runs from southern North America to the central part of Central America. Jade is a common resource. So are basalt and obsidian, which are types of black rocks formed from lava. Some Mesoamerican peoples carved huge statues out of basalt. Others made arrowheads and knives from obsidian. Mesoamerica is a rugged, or rough, land. There are two mountain ranges in northern Mesoamerica. These are the Sierra Madre Occidental and the Sierra Madre Oriental. The Plateau of Mexico sits between these ranges. A plateau is a high, flat area. Volcanoes are south of the plateau. They produce fertile soil for farming. South of the volcanoes are highlands. This rugged area has ridges and gorges. The climate of Mesoamerica changes depending on where you are. Some places are dry deserts. In other places enough rain falls for crops and forests to grow. Mesoamericans have grown maize (corn), beans, and squash for thousands of years.

A Land of Lush Coasts

The interior of Mesoamerica is a land of rugged mountains and plateaus. Mesoamerica also has long coastlines. No place in Mesoamerica is farther than about 200 miles from the coast. The Gulf of Mexico is to the north. Much of the land near the gulf's coast is covered with tropical rain forest. The climate is hot and humid. There are also grasslands, swamps, and rivers. The Yucatán Peninsula forms the southeastern border of the Gulf of Mexico. A **peninsula** is an arm of land sticking into the sea so that it is nearly surrounded by water. The Yucatán Peninsula has few rivers. But it does have many underground streams and caves. The roofs of many of these underground streams have collapsed and created **cenotes,** or natural wells. Cenotes were used as sources of drinking water. The southwest coastline of Mesoamerica sits on the Pacific Ocean. It is a mountainous area.

A Land of Many Peoples

Many peoples lived in Mesoamerica. Its different environments and climates helped them develop different cultures. Yet the peoples of Mesoamerica had many things in common. They all had advanced forms of agriculture. They grew crops such as beans, maize, chili peppers, and squash. Many people lived in rural areas. Others lived in cities and towns. Cities contained temple-pyramids and large works of art such as stone monuments. People developed very accurate calendars. They also used hieroglyphic writing different from that of other civilizations.

© Scott Foresman 6

Lesson 1: Review

1. 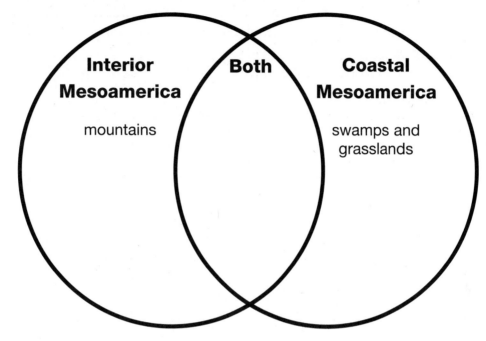 **Compare and Contrast** Fill in the missing comparisons.

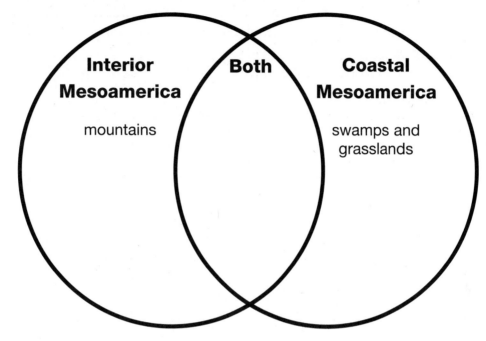

Interior Mesoamerica

mountains

Both

Coastal Mesoamerica

swamps and grasslands

2. Where is Mesoamerica?

_____

_____

3. What were three crops the Mesoamericans grew?

_____

_____

4. How did the early peoples of Mesoamerica use the natural resources of the region?

_____

_____

5. **Critical Thinking:** *Make Inferences* How do you think the environments described in this lesson would influence the Mesoamerican peoples? Use the word **peninsula** in your answer.

_____

_____

Lesson 2: The Olmec and the Maya

Vocabulary

theocracy a government in which the leader and the ruling classes are believed to represent the will of the gods

aqueduct a structure that carries flowing water

codex a book with screens that fold together

A Mother Civilization

The Olmec civilization was Mesoamerica's first great civilization. It lasted from about 1200 B.C. to about 300 B.C. The Olmec lived on the coast of the Gulf of Mexico. Most Olmec were farmers, but they also hunted and fished. They lived in small houses that surrounded small villages. The Olmec people were divided into social classes based on wealth and power. The Olmec government was a **theocracy.** Priests and government officials made up the most powerful social class. Merchants and craftspeople made up other social classes. Farmers made up the lowest. Olmec villages were connected by roads. The Olmec traveled these roads and traded with other Mesoamerican peoples. The Olmec civilization is often called "the Mother Civilization" of Mesoamerica. This is because the Olmec influenced all of the later Mesoamerican civilizations.

Olmec Accomplishments

The Olmec are most famous for the giant stone heads they made. The huge heads often represented Olmec rulers. The Olmec also made sculptures of their gods. The Olmec developed a number system, a calendar, and a form of writing. Later Mesoamerican civilizations would learn from the Olmec's developments. No one knows why the Olmec civilization disappeared. Some people believe that the Olmec were the ancestors of the Maya.

The Maya

The Maya lived in more than 100 locations in Central America and Mexico. A large part of their civilization was on the Yucatán Peninsula, close to where the Olmec had lived. Mayan civilization was at its strongest about A.D. 250 and continued for another 650 years. The city-state Tikal was once home to nearly 100,000 Maya. More than 3,000 structures were built there. Today this ancient city has ruins of palaces, baths, pyramids, and **aqueducts.** Aqueducts carried running water. As sources of water, cenotes were holy to the Maya. Cenotes were sinkholes that collected water. Like the Olmec, the Maya developed a form of writing and lived in a theocracy. Also both Olmec and Mayan cities were set up to honor the gods.

Time and Numbers

The Maya used calendars to write down birth dates, marriages, and other important information. The Maya actually had two different calendars. One was for the seasons. The other was for religious ceremonies. The Maya used a **codex,** or folding-screen book, to write down information forecasting the future. Codexes also contained information about religious ceremonies. A codex was made of fig leaf bark or animal skin. The Maya were great mathematicians. They created their own counting system.

Daily Life

Entire families lived together in Mayan culture. Men farmed and hunted. Women did housekeeping chores and made clothing. Houses were small and made of adobe, or dried mud-bricks. The Maya began to leave their cities about A.D. 900. Today some descendants of the Maya live in Mexico and Guatemala. But no one knows what happened to Mayan civilization.

© Scott Foresman 6

Lesson 2: Review

1. ⟲ **Compare and Contrast** Complete the diagram to compare and contrast the Olmec and the Maya.

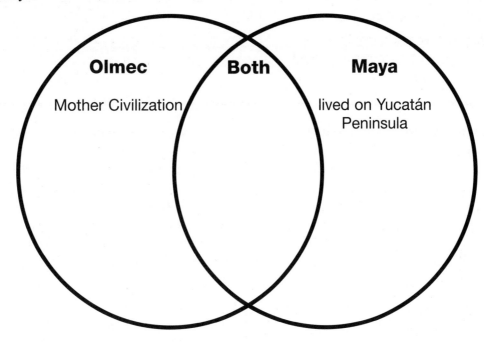

Olmec

Mother Civilization

Both

Maya

lived on Yucatán Peninsula

2. Why is the Olmec culture called a "Mother Civilization"?

_____

_____

3. Why were cenotes important to the Maya?

_____

_____

4. How were the Olmec and Mayan civilizations organized? Use the word **theocracy** in your answer.

_____

_____

5. **Critical Thinking:** *Make Inferences* Do you think it is likely that the Olmec were the ancestors of the Maya? Why or why not?

_____

_____

Lesson 3: The Aztecs

Vocabulary

mercenary a hired soldier
chinampa a human-made island
causeway a raised bridge made of land
alliance an agreement to work with others

A Mesoamerican Civilization

The Aztec civilization was the last great civilization of Mesoamerica. The Aztec economy was based on farming. The Aztecs built many great structures out of stone. They also were astronomers and developed a form of writing. They worshipped many gods. Unlike other Mesoamerican civilizations, the Aztecs built a great empire.

Early Aztec History

The Aztecs once called themselves the Mexica. At first they were just one of many Mesoamerican peoples. The Mexica sometimes served as **mercenaries,** or hired soldiers. Other times they lived under the rule of others. In the mid-1300s, the Mexica started the city of Tenochtitlan in present-day Mexico. It was built on two swampy islands in the middle of Lake Texcoco. To make more room as the city grew, the Mexica built **chinampas,** or islands. They made chinampas by piling up mud and plants in the lake. The chinampas were used as farmland. The chinampas, natural islands, and the mainland were connected by **causeways**. Causeways are raised bridges made of land. Tenochtitlan soon became a powerful city-state. The Mexica formed **alliances,** or agreements, with neighboring city-states. These alliances helped the Mexica conquer other city-states. The Mexica started calling themselves the Aztecs after their legendary homeland, Aztlán. The Aztec Empire had begun.

The Aztec Empire

At its peak, Tenochtitlan had a population of 300,000 people. The Aztecs controlled many city-states. The population of the entire Aztec Empire may have been as many as 5 million people. The empire collected taxes from the people it conquered and became rich. The Aztecs gained such a large empire because warfare was a normal part of life for them. All young men were trained to fight in battles. Those who showed bravery in battle became famous.

Life

Religion was very important to Aztec life. The Aztecs worshipped hundreds of gods and goddesses. The god Quetzalcóatl was the god of creation. The Aztecs had religious ceremonies that were based on agricultural events. These events included planting and harvesting. The Aztecs performed many human sacrifices to honor their gods. The Aztecs mostly sacrificed people captured in war. Yet they sometimes sacrificed their own people.

A Violent End

The Aztecs were a conquering people. But in the end the Aztecs themselves were conquered. In 1502 Moctezuma II became emperor. For the next two decades, the Aztec Empire was at its height. In 1519 Spanish explorers led by Hernando Cortés marched into Tenochtitlan. The Aztecs did not fight him and his men at first. The Aztecs might have thought he was the god Quetzalcóatl. The Aztecs began to fight when they realized that Cortés wanted to conquer them. But they were not successful. By 1521 the Spanish had conquered the Aztec Empire.

Lesson 3: Review

1. **Main Idea and Details** Complete the diagram below.

The Aztecs built a great empire.

The Aztecs formed alliances with other city-states.

The Aztecs conquered other city-states.

2. What was Tenochtitlan?

_____

_____

_____

3. How did the Aztecs use alliances to build their empire?

_____

_____

_____

4. What became of the Aztec Empire?

_____

_____

_____

5. **Critical Thinking:** *Make Inferences* Do you think the Aztec Empire would have continued without the arrival of the Spanish?

_____

_____

_____

Lesson 1: Geography of South America

Vocabulary

wetland an area of very moist soil, such as a swamp

biome a place that has a particular climate and types of plants and animals

scrub land an area where plants grow low

archipelago a group of islands

A Land of World Records

South America is a land of world records. It has the world's highest waterfall, Angel Falls. It has the world's second longest river, the Amazon River. It has the world's largest rain forest, the Amazon rain forest. It has the world's largest **wetland,** the Pantanal. And it has the world's longest mountain chain, the 4,500-mile-long Andes Mountains. High in the mountains there are glaciers. People have lived in the harsh Andes for thousands of years, including on the Altiplano. The Altiplano is a region of high plains and plateaus. People could farm potatoes, grain, and maize (corn) in this cold, dry place. Two animals, the llama and the alpaca, were first domesticated on the Altiplano.

Lake Titicaca

Lake Titicaca lies on the Altiplano in the present-day countries of Bolivia and Peru. Some ruins at Lake Titicaca are more than 2,000 years old. Lake Titicaca has a mild climate. One advantage of living near the lake is that many rivers flow into the lake. These rivers provide fresh water and fish. The land near the lake can grow crops such as maize, potatoes, and barley. Reeds grow at the edge of the lake. People have been using the reeds to make boats to sail on the lake since ancient times.

Many Landscapes

South America is home to many different kinds of **biomes.** Biomes are places with their own type of climate and own types of plants and animals. Grasslands, deserts, and rain forests are types of biomes. The Andes Mountains run along the western edge of South America. They run through both the northern and southern parts of the continent. The Amazon River is in the north. The river drains the Amazon rain forest. The Eastern Highlands are mountains in the northeast. Also in this region are the Guiana Highlands, a land of tropical forests. Central and southern South America are different. This area is a land of plains. The Atacama Desert is in the northern part of the present-day country of Chile. Much of southern and central South America is **scrub land,** or an area where plants grow low to the ground. The Pampas, a huge grassland, sits at the southern end of the plains. The southern tip of South America is made up of an **archipelago,** or group of islands. It is called Tierra del Fuego.

The Peoples of South America

People have lived in all of the different regions of South America. Only a few of the early peoples created large civilizations. This may be because mountains and forests separated people from one another. Yet a civilization did grow in a surprising place, the rugged Andes Mountains.

Lesson 1: Review

1. 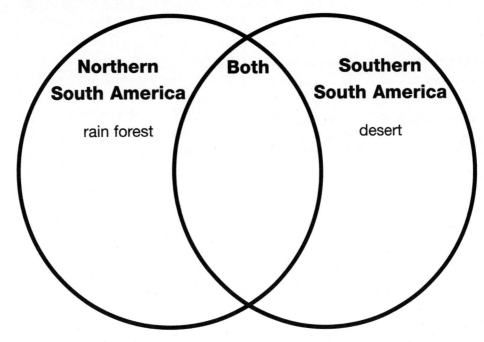 **Compare and Contrast** Complete the diagram below.

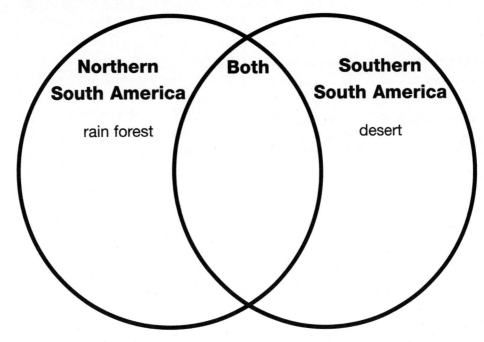

Northern South America

rain forest

Both

Southern South America

desert

2. What world record is held by the Andes Mountains?

_____

_____

3. Why did ancient peoples settle near Lake Titicaca?

_____

_____

4. What are several types of landscapes that can be found in South America? Use the word **biome** in your answer.

_____

_____

5. Critical Thinking: *Make Generalizations* In which part of South America do you think it would be easiest for people to live? Why?

_____

_____

Lesson 2: The Chavín and the Mochica

The Chavín

From about 900 B.C. to 200 B.C., the Chavín civilization lived in the Andes Mountains in the present-day country of Peru. The Chavín lived here even though Peru is a rough land. Its coasts are dry and its mountains are high. We know about the civilization because of its ruins, especially the city of Chavín. The Chavín were great artists. Today they are famous for their art. They made textiles, pottery, and stone carvings. The Chavín style of art is known for its pictures of jaguars, crocodiles, and serpents. Some people think that the Chavín worshipped jaguars. Archaeologists have found Chavín art over a large area. This may mean that the Chavín influenced and brought together the other peoples living in the area. No one knows why the Chavín suddenly disappeared. After the Chavín vanished, the ancient people of Peru split into many cultures. They would not come together for another 500 years.

The Mochica

The Mochica civilization began about A.D. 100 in today's Peru. It lasted for about 700 years. These people are called the Mochica because their artifacts have been found in the Moche Valley. Like the Chavín before them, the Mochica lived in river valleys between the mountains of Peru. The Mochica were great artists too. They left behind ceramic pots, woven textiles, murals, and amazing metal objects. The Mochica were also skilled fishermen, builders, and farmers. They irrigated their crops with the water that flowed down from the Andes. Mochica city-states had pyramids, stone courtyards, and plazas. The ruins of these city-states tell much about Mochica life. Water jars were painted with pictures of gods and ceremonies. These pictures give us information about Mochica religion. The disappearance of the Mochica remains a mystery.

Solving a Mystery

Archaeologists are still finding artifacts from these two civilizations. Every new artifact tells us a little more about these people's lives. The Andes Mountains might not seem to be a good place for an empire to begin. But hundreds of years after the Mochica disappeared, a great empire did begin in this region.

Lesson 2: Review

1. **Main Idea and Details** Complete the diagram below.

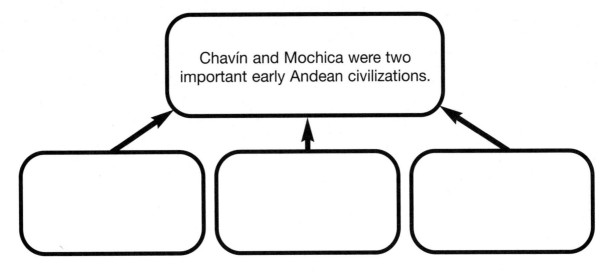

Chavín and Mochica were two important early Andean civilizations.

2. Where did the Chavín and Mochica live?

_____

_____

_____

3. Describe Chavín art and explain how it has helped us learn about Chavín culture.

_____

_____

_____

4. How do we know about the Chavín and the Mochica?

_____

_____

_____

5. **Critical Thinking:** *Accuracy of Information* Do the artifacts that archaeologists have found tell us how the Chavín and Mochica disappeared? Explain your answer.

_____

_____

_____

Lesson 3: The Inca

Vocabulary

quipu a rope with different lengths and colors of knotted cord used to keep track of things

A Vast Empire

The Inca Empire was the largest and richest empire the Americas had ever seen. The empire stretched down the western side of the Andes. It included dozens of different peoples. Little is known about the Inca's beginnings. Much of what we do know comes from the archaeological site of Machu Picchu. It was a mountaintop city that may have been home to about 1,000 people. Many buildings there were temples. The city may have been a religious center. Cuzco was the Inca capital. About A.D. 1200, the Inca civilization was not very large. But by conquering some neighboring peoples and forming alliances with others, the empire became huge.

An Empire Is Born

A man named Pachacuti may have been the main reason the Inca built a huge empire. In 1438 a people called the Chancas attacked the Inca. The Inca ruler, Viracocha, ran away. But one of his sons, Pachacuti, stayed to fight. Pachacuti defeated the Chancas and became the Inca emperor, or ruler. He expanded the Inca territory by conquering nearby peoples. Conquered men became Inca soldiers. The Inca army grew in size and strength. Pachacuti also was a great builder. Under his leadership many buildings went up in Cuzco. In 1471 Pachacuti's son, Topa Inca, became emperor. Topa Inca conquered many peoples in the region. He nearly doubled the size of the Inca Empire.

Empire Builders

The huge Inca Empire held together because of smart government. When the Inca conquered a people, they allowed the old ruler to stay in power as long as he was loyal to the Inca. Conquered rulers then had little reason to fight the Inca, although they did pay taxes to the Inca. The Inca government carefully watched over the people in the empire. There was a chain of command. It included the ministers of the empire, the traveling inspectors, and the governors of the provinces. Each governor was in charge of about 10,000 Inca subjects, as well as other government workers. When the emperor gave an order, it went down the chain of command to everyone in the empire. The Inca never developed a system of writing. But they did use **quipu,** or knotted cords, to keep records for many things. We have learned about the Inca government from quipu. The Inca also were good stoneworkers. They cut stones and fit them together so well that they did not need to use cement.

Inca Roads

The Inca built excellent roads. In fact, they built more than 14,000 miles of roads to link together the empire. The Inca did not use wheels to move things, so their roads did not have to be of a certain width. Some roads were not much more than footpaths. Others were wide and paved. Inca roads were used by only the government and army. Some roads are still around today.

The Inca Legacy

The Inca Empire did not last very long. Yet their ruins show us that their cities were magnificent. In 1527 civil war broke out in the Inca Empire. Just as the war was ending, the Spanish explorer Francisco Pizarro arrived. He had only 167 men. But he did have horses and guns. This helped him conquer the already weakened Inca Empire.

Lesson 3: Review

1. **Main Idea and Details** List some of the main accomplishments of the Inca in the boxes below.

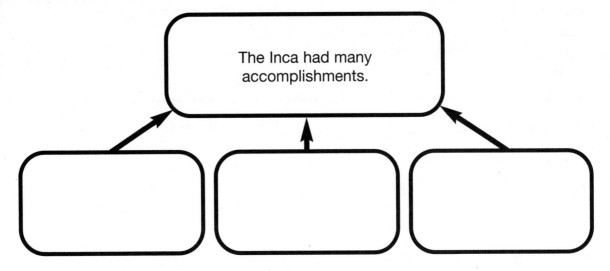

The Inca had many accomplishments.

2. Who was Pachacuti?

_____

_____

_____

3. What was the Inca capital?

_____

_____

_____

4. How did the Inca system of government help hold the empire together? Use the word **quipu** in your answer.

_____

_____

_____

5. **Critical Thinking:** *Make Inferences* Do you think the Inca roads would have been built differently if the Inca had used wheels for transport? Explain your answer.

_____

_____

_____

Lesson 1: Geography of North America

Vocabulary

basin and range a region that has both low areas and small mountain ranges
tributary a smaller stream or river that flows into a larger river
tundra a type of cold, treeless land with only low-lying plants
arid dry

A Diverse Land

North America has many different landscapes. There are tall mountains and deep valleys. There are forests, deserts, beaches, grasslands, and cold regions. The Rocky Mountains, or "the Rockies," stretch almost the entire length of North America. The Rockies are young mountains. They have tall, sharp peaks. To the west is an area of **basins and ranges** often called the Great Basin. Low areas and small mountain ranges make up this area. Far to the east are the Appalachian Mountains. They are older than the Rockies. The Appalachians are low, rounded mountains. Forested valleys divide these mountains. The Interior Plains is toward the center of the country. In ancient times the eastern Interior Plains was covered with forests. The western part of the plains is called the Great Plains. It is grassland, much as it was in ancient times. The Interior Plains region is home to the great Mississippi River and its **tributaries.** A tributary is a smaller stream or river that flows into a larger river. Evergreen forests cover the Canadian Shield, which is north of the Interior Plains. The Coastal Lowlands is south of the Interior Plains and the Appalachians. This is a low, humid area. North America has the longest coastline of all the continents.

Diverse Climate

North America has about ten different climate regions. These range from cold and dry to hot and wet. In the north the climate is subarctic. Much of the land is **tundra.** Tundra is a type of cold, treeless land. It is cold year-round, and not much plant life grows. In the west the climate is more **arid,** or dry. The eastern and southern climates are more tropical and humid. There is more plant life in these areas. Summers are longer, and winters are shorter. In between the northern and southern regions the climates are more moderate. They are usually not very cold or very hot. Yet thunderstorms, blizzards, and tornadoes can occur in these areas.

Many Peoples

The original people living in North America were American Indians, or Native Americans. There were hundreds of different cultural groups. Each had its own name. They adapted to the many different climates and landscapes of North America.

Lesson 1: Review

1. 🔄 **Compare and Contrast** Complete the diagram below by comparing the Rocky and Appalachian Mountains.

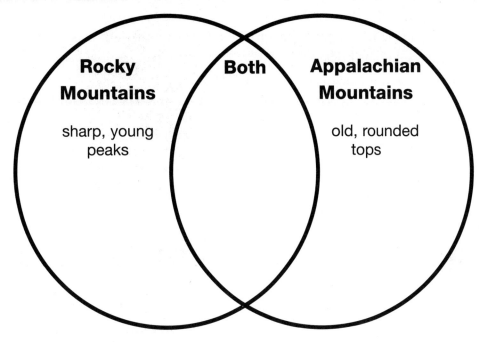

Rocky Mountains

sharp, young peaks

Both

Appalachian Mountains

old, rounded tops

2. How were the eastern Interior Plains different in ancient times?

_____

_____

3. How would you describe the climate of North America?

_____

_____

4. What are several types of landscapes that can be found in North America?

_____

_____

5. **Critical Thinking:** *Make Inferences* How would the diverse landscapes of North America influence the cultures that developed there? Use two vocabulary words from the lesson in your answer.

_____

_____

Lesson 2: The Southwestern Peoples

Vocabulary

etching a way of making a printed design
pit house a house made from a pit in the ground that is covered with logs, plants, and mud
pueblo a structure of adobe bricks
adobe a building material made from sun-dried mud

The Vanished Ones

Etching was developed in what is now the southwestern United States. We do not know the name of the people who developed this type of art. But a later culture called them the Hohokam, which meant "the Vanished Ones." The Hohokam lived in present-day Arizona from about A.D. 300 until about 1400. The Hohokam survived the harsh desert climate by farming. They used irrigation to water their fields. Farming made villages possible. The Hohokam lived in **pit houses.** Pit houses are made by digging a hole in the ground. The pit gave the Hohokam relief from the hot sun. At Hohokam villages, people made pottery and human figures from clay. People also made copper bells and mirrors from polished iron. No one knows why the Hohokam left their villages and vanished.

The Ancient Ones

The Anasazi thrived from about A.D. 100 to 1280. *Anasazi* is the Navajo word for "the Ancient Ones." The Anasazi also lived in the Southwest. Some of their descendants, or people born into the same family, live in the region today. The Anasazi lived in **pueblos,** or structures made of adobe bricks. **Adobe** is made from sun-dried mud. Pueblos are large buildings several stories high. Their thick walls blocked out sunlight and kept in cool air. They have many rooms. One of these pueblos, called Pueblo Bonito, was five stories tall with 800 rooms. Archaeologists study the pueblos to learn more about the Anasazi. Many pueblos may have been used as forts. The

Anasazi were great farmers. They brought water to their crops using irrigation. They also may have collected rainwater. The Anasazi made beautiful pottery, jewelry, and baskets. They could communicate using signal fires. The Anasazi might have left their pueblos because of a long drought, or period of little rainfall.

Contact Among Peoples

Ancient Native American cultures were connected to one another. First, they were all influenced by the cultures of the past. Second, they all had contact with other cultures. Sometimes the cultures fought. Sometimes the cultures were friendly with each other. The groups shared ideas and may have traded with each other.

© Scott Foresman 6

Lesson 2: Review

1. ⟳ **Compare and Contrast** Complete the diagram below by contrasting the Hohokam and the Anasazi cultures.

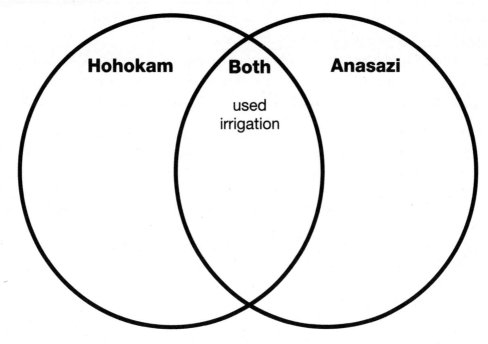

Hohokam   **Both**   **Anasazi**

used irrigation

2. What art technique did the Hohokam invent?

_____

_____

3. What are pueblos?

_____

_____

4. How did the Hohokam and the Anasazi farm desert land?

_____

_____

5. **Critical Thinking:** *Evaluate Information* Which is better suited to life in a hot and arid environment: a pit house or a pueblo? Explain your answer.

_____

_____

© Scott Foresman 6

Lesson 3: The Mound Builders

Vocabulary

burial mound a human-made mound in which many people are buried

wattle a house frame made of twigs, logs, branches, or vines

wigwam a dome-shaped house made of branches covered with animal skins or woven mats

temple mound a human-made mound used for religious purposes or ceremonies

The Adena Culture

Across the eastern United States are great mounds of earth. They can be found in Illinois, Ohio, Florida, Canada, and the Great Lakes area. They were built by different Native American cultures. Together these cultures are called the mound builders. The Adena culture was one of the first mound builders groups. The Adena culture developed in the Ohio River Valley. They built **burial mounds.** One of the largest is the Great Serpent Mound in what is now Ohio. The Adena thrived from about 700 B.C. to about A.D. 100. They were hunter-gatherers, but they did farm a little. They lived in small circular houses that had frames called **wattles.** The Adena disappeared suddenly. No one knows why.

The Hopewell Culture

The Hopewell culture was very similar to the Adena culture. The Hopewell also built burial mounds and were hunter-gatherers. They lived in small houses that were like **wigwams,** dome-shaped frames made of branches. However, the Hopewell lived in a much larger area than the Adena, from the Great Lakes to the Gulf Coast. The Hopewell also farmed more than the Adena. They also built more mounds, which were larger and more complex. Unlike the Adena, the Hopewell traded over a large area. The Hopewell thrived from about 100 B.C. to about A.D. 500. Like the Adena, no one knows why the Hopewell disappeared.

Mississippian Culture

The Mississippian culture lived in much the same area as the Hopewell after about A.D. 700. The Mississippian people built mounds, but they were **temple mounds.** These mounds were used for religious purposes or ceremonies. Cahokia is the largest temple mound site, with 85 mounds. It still stands in present-day Illinois, near St. Louis, Missouri. It covers an area the size of 15 football fields and stands more than 100 feet high!

Lesson 3: Review

1. ⟳ **Compare and Contrast** Complete the diagram below by contrasting the Adena and Hopewell cultures.

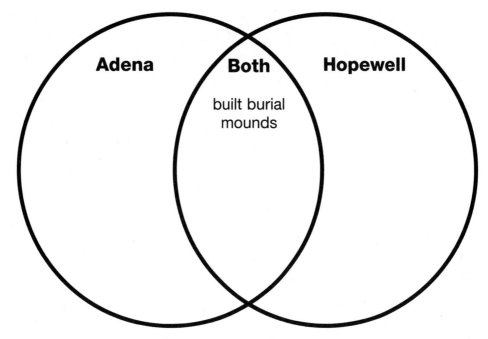

Adena   **Both**   **Hopewell**

built burial
mounds

2. Why did the Adena people build mounds?

_____

_____

3. Why did the Mississippian people build mounds?

_____

_____

4. Where can some of the remains of mound-building cultures be found today?

_____

_____

5. **Critical Thinking:** *Make Inferences* Cahokia is home to 85 large mounds. What can you conclude about the people who lived in Cahokia based on this fact alone?

_____

_____

Name _____ Date _____

Lesson 4: Early Canadians

Vocabulary

snowhouse a temporary shelter made of blocks of snow
sod house a house made of blocks of soil and plants cut from frozen ground
long house a rectangular building made of logs and covered with bark

Survivors in the Arctic

Northern Canada is very cold and has few natural resources. Still, the early peoples who lived there knew how to survive. The Inuit probably first came to northern Canada about 5,000 years ago. There were few plants, so the Inuit hunted and fished. They hunted birds, whales, and polar bears. Most of what they needed came from caribou and seal. Both animals provided meat and blood for food. Their skins and fur were used for clothing and blankets. Their bones were carved into artwork and tools. Seal intestines were used for waterproof jackets and boat covers. Some Inuit lived in **snowhouses,** or igloos. Most lived in **sod houses,** which were built out of blocks of soil and plants. The Inuit still live in Canada today.

The Iroquois and Algonquin

The Iroquois lived far to the south of the Inuit. They were members of the Iroquois-speaking Native American peoples. These peoples all lived in similar ways around the eastern Great Lakes. The Iroquois became skilled at farming around A.D. 1000. They began to live in more permanent villages. Many families lived together in **long houses.** The frames of these houses were made of logs and covered by bark. Some houses were more than 100 feet long! The Algonquin people lived near the Ottawa River in east-central Canada. They belonged to a larger group of Algonquin-speaking peoples. The Algonquin grew some crops, but they were mainly hunters. Their forested homeland had many deer and moose. They also fished and gathered plants. The Algonquin lived in lodges made of small logs and bark.

© Scott Foresman 6

Lesson 4: Review

1. **Compare and Contrast** Complete the diagram by contrasting the Inuit and the Algonquin.

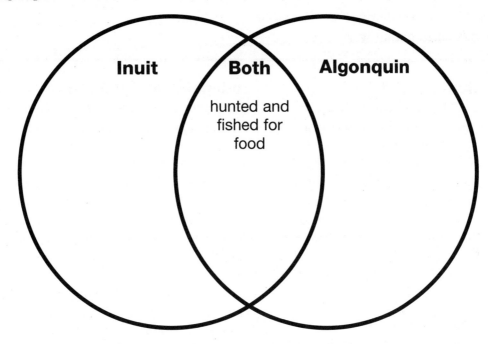

Inuit   **Both**   **Algonquin**

hunted and
fished for
food

2. What did the Inuit use seals for?

_____

_____

3. Where did the Iroquois peoples live?

_____

_____

4. How did the Iroquois and Algonquin use forest resources to build their homes?

_____

_____

5. **Critical Thinking:** *Make Inferences* Why do you think the Algonquin peoples did not become dedicated to farming?

_____

_____

© Scott Foresman 6

Lesson 1: The Geography of Greece

Vocabulary

agora   an outdoor marketplace in ancient Greece
plunder   goods taken during war

A Mountainous Land

Many ancient civilizations formed near rivers. The rivers would overflow in the spring and make the soil good for farming. Greece did not depend on a river. Greece is a rugged, mountainous land with no great rivers. It does not have much good farmland. Greece is located in the southeastern corner of Europe. It is on the southern tip of the Balkan Peninsula. Greek-speaking people also lived on islands in the Aegean Sea. The sea separates Greece from the western edge of Asia.

A Land Tied to the Sea

Greece is surrounded by the sea on three sides. The Aegean Sea is to the east. The Ionian Sea is to the west. This sea separates Greece from Italy. The Mediterranean Sea is to the south. It links Greece with Asia, North Africa, and the western part of Europe. Greece's coastline has many excellent harbors. The Greeks were great sailors and traders. Most people in ancient Greece lived along the coast and in the land's few river valleys. There the Greeks raised animals and grew crops such as grapes, olives, and barley. The Greeks traded with other peoples across the seas. Trade allowed Greek ideas to spread. It also allowed the Greeks to learn from other cultures.

Independent Communities

Geography affected how life in Greece developed. Uniting the country under one government was difficult. Ancient Greeks did share the same language and religion. Mountains divided Greece into different regions and kept people apart. Therefore, many independent cities sprang up. Each city did things its own way. The climate of Greece is pleasant, and the Greeks had an outdoor way of life. The **agora,** or outdoor marketplace, was common in cities. The Greeks watched plays in outdoor theaters. Political meetings, religious celebrations, and sports contests also were held outdoors.

Two Early Greek Civilizations

The Minoan civilization was on the island of Crete, in the Mediterranean Sea. By 2500 B.C., the Minoans had a written language. They also could weave cloth and make pottery and jewelry. The Minoans controlled trade in the Aegean Sea. By 1600 B.C., the Minoans were powerful. Minoan ships protected the kingdom from invaders. Then the Minoan civilization grew weak. No one knows why. About 2000 B.C., groups of people went to the Greek mainland. Over hundreds of years, new city-states sprang up. The greatest early city-state was Mycenae. It became the center of civilization in the eastern Mediterranean. Mycenae was powerful and well defended. Its ships captured the ships of other cities. The Myceneans took **plunder,** or goods taken during war.

© Scott Foresman 6

Lesson 1: Review

1. 🔄 **Main Idea and Details** Write an appropriate main idea in the box for the three supporting details shown below.

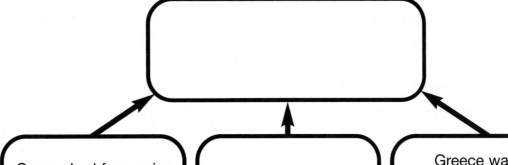

2. What was the Minoan civilization?

_____

_____

3. What are the three seas that border Greece?

_____

_____

4. What effect did mountains have on the peoples in Greece?

_____

_____

5. **Critical Thinking:** *Make Generalizations* In your own words, describe the importance of the sea to the people of Greece.

_____

_____

Lesson 2: The Greek City-States

Vocabulary

myth a traditional story that may be about gods and goddesses

immortal able to live forever

aristocracy a government controlled by a few wealthy families

democracy a government run by the people

The Power of Greek Myths and Legends

The Trojan War was fought between the Greeks and the people of Troy, a city in western Asia. The story of the war is a blend of myth and legend. **Myths** are stories that may be about gods and goddesses. Legends are stories about heroes. Gods and goddesses helped heroes on both sides of the Trojan War. The ancient Greeks tried to keep their gods and goddesses happy. The war started when Helen was carried off from the city-state of Sparta to Troy. To end the war, the Greeks built a giant, wooden horse. The Trojans thought it was a gift and pulled the horse into the city. Greek soldiers were hiding in the horse. They opened the gates of Troy for the Greek army. Homer composed two poems about the war—the *Iliad* and the *Odyssey*. Myths and legends were passed down by word of mouth.

The Gods of Mount Olympus

The Greeks developed many myths. Myths helped them explain things that happen in nature and life. The Greeks thought that most gods lived on Mount Olympus, in northern Greece. They thought that their gods were **immortal,** or able to live forever. The Greeks also believed that their gods had special powers. The Greeks held athletic contests every four years to honor Zeus, the king of the gods. The contests, held in the city of Olympia, became known as the Olympic Games.

Democracy Begins in Greece

Kings ruled some Greek city-states. In others, the government was an **aristocracy.** It was controlled by rich families. Around 500 B.C., democracy began to develop in some city-states. **Democracy** is a government run by the people. The city-state of Athens was governed by the Assembly. The Assembly was made up of all citizens older than 18. Later 500 citizens were chosen to serve on a council for a year. The Assembly had to approve the council's decisions. Only citizens could be part of the Greek democracy. Slaves, women, and workers born outside of Athens were not considered citizens. They could not own property, vote, or testify in court.

Rivals: Athens and Sparta

The citizens of Athens had to defend the city during conflicts and take part in government. The city-state of Sparta was a military state. It conquered other city-states and forced their people to become slaves. The army was the center of life. Only healthy babies were allowed to live. At seven years old, Spartan boys began difficult training for a life in the army.

Women in Sparta

Sparta expected its women to be strong and responsible. Spartan women played many sports. They wanted their sons to fight bravely in battle. Spartan women had more rights than women in other city-states. They could own property. However, they could not take part in government.

© Scott Foresman 6

Lesson 2: Review

1. **Compare and Contrast** Compare and contrast Athens and Sparta.

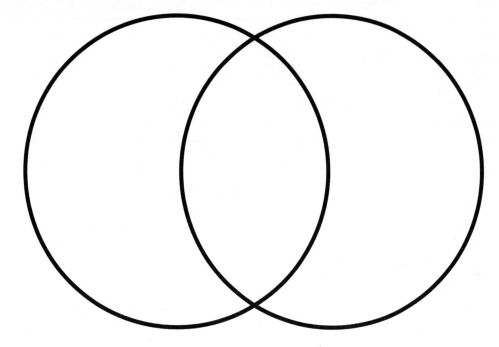

2. Where did the Greeks believe that most gods lived?

_____

_____

3. What is an aristocracy?

_____

_____

4. What does the story of the Trojan War tell us about the Greek attitudes toward their gods and goddesses?

_____

_____

5. **Critical Thinking:** *Evaluate Information* If you had the choice, would you rather grow up in Athens or in Sparta? Why?

_____

_____

© Scott Foresman 6

Lesson 3: The Golden Age of Athens

Vocabulary

marathon a long race based on an ancient Greek legend

philosopher a person who studies truth and knowledge

reason logical thinking

plague a fast-spreading disease that is often deadly

mercenary a hired soldier

The Greeks Clash with the Persians

In 490 B.C., Persia attacked the Greek mainland with a huge army. Persia was the most powerful empire of its time. The Persian and Athenian armies battled on a plain northeast of Athens called Marathon. The Athenians won. According to legend, a warrior ran 25 miles to Athens with the news. Today the **marathon** is a long race based on the Greek legend. The Athenians and the Spartans were enemies. But they knew the Persians would attack again. They joined forces to fight the Persians. In 480 B.C., the Athenian ships destroyed the Persian fleet in the Battle of Salamis. This battle ended the war.

The Golden Age

After defeating the Persians, Athens entered a period known as the Golden Age. Athens built beautiful new temples, statues, and monuments. Greek **philosophers** such as Socrates, Plato, and Aristotle studied truth and knowledge. Greek philosophers respected **reason,** or logical thinking. They thought people could figure out why things happened in nature. They did not think things happened just because the gods caused them to. Greek physicians studied the causes of sickness.

The Greeks Fight Against Each Other

Athens was the most powerful Greek city-state during the Golden Age. Athenian leaders formed an alliance, or group that works together, called the Delian League. The Athenians forced some city-states to join the League. They used the League's money to put up buildings in Athens. This angered other city-states. Sparta led the angry city-states. A war between Sparta and Athens began in 431 B.C. It was called the Peloponnesian War. Sparta had great power on the land. Athens' navy had great power on the sea. This made it hard for either city-state to win the war. Then a **plague** broke out in Athens. A plague is a deadly, fast-spreading disease. The plague killed thousands of people including the leader of Athens. Athens surrendered in 404 B.C.

Decline of the Greek City-States

In Greece, hard times followed the war. Many young Greek men became **mercenaries,** or hired soldiers, in the Persian army. Athens regained its strength in trade, but all of Greece was weakened. Sparta had lost many soldiers in the war. In 371 B.C., Sparta lost a battle against the Greek city Thebes. Macedonia was to the north of Greece. Macedonia grew in power and became a threat to Greece.

© Scott Foresman 6

Lesson 3: Review

1. ⟳ **Main Idea and Details** Fill in the missing main idea in the blank box.

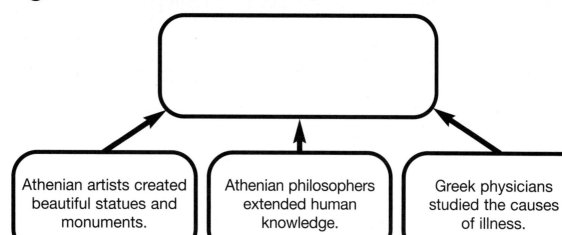

2. What was the Delian League?

_____

_____

_____

3. Why was the Battle of Salamis important to Greece?

_____

_____

_____

4. What were some of the fields of study in which Athens excelled during its Golden Age?

_____

_____

_____

5. **Critical Thinking: *Solve Complex Problems*** What advice would you have given to the leaders of Athens that might have helped them avoid the problems that developed? Use the word **reason** in your answer.

_____

_____

_____

Lesson 4: Alexander the Great

Alexander's Conquests

Philip II was the king of Macedonia. After he was killed, his 20-year-old son Alexander became king. Two years later, in 334 B.C., Alexander invaded the Persian Empire. During a major battle, Alexander told his army not to retreat from the larger Persian army. He showed his leadership by ordering his army to attack the Persians. The Persians ran away. Alexander's army had won. Alexander then conquered Syria and Phoenicia. Alexander also took over Egypt and was crowned pharaoh.

A Great Empire

In 331 B.C., Alexander's army fought and beat the larger Persian army again. Alexander then led his army eastward. The army won every battle it fought. Five years after his march started, the soldiers were in India. They were very tired and ready to stop fighting. Alexander marched his army back toward Greece. He died on the way back. The empire he created was huge. It spread across Europe, Asia, and Africa. During his nearly 13 years in power, Alexander spread Greek culture. He also took on many Asian ways. A new civilization rose from this blend of Greek and Asian cultures. We call this period the Hellenistic Age. The young king is remembered as "Alexander the Great."

The Hellenistic Age

After Alexander's death three of his generals divided the empire among themselves. For 300 years, Hellenistic culture spread. New cities were founded in Europe, northern Africa, and western Asia. The cities became centers of Greek culture. Trade grew between Hellenistic cities and far-off parts of the world. Alexandria was a city in Egypt. It became the greatest center of trade and learning. It had the busiest port of its time and a great library.

Discovery and Invention

During the Hellenistic Age, Greek science and mathematics reached their peaks. Hippocrates was a doctor who looked for natural causes of diseases. Today he is often called the father of medicine. He believed a good diet and lifestyle were needed for good health. Archimedes was a famous inventor and mathematician. He made discoveries about levers. He also improved pulleys for carrying heavy objects. Pythagoras was a mathematician whose ideas about numbers led to the study of geometry. Euclid was the most important mathematician of his time. Students today still study his system of plane geometry.

Lesson 4: Review

1. **Cause and Effect** Fill in the missing causes and effect.

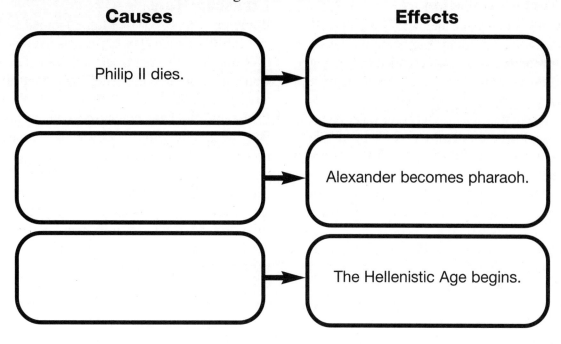

Causes		Effects

Philip II dies.

Alexander becomes pharaoh.

The Hellenistic Age begins.

2. How did Alexander become king of Macedonia?

_____

_____

3. How did Alexander display his leadership qualities?

_____

_____

4. What was Hellenistic culture, and how did it begin?

_____

_____

5. **Critical Thinking:** *Solve Complex Problems* How might the discoveries made by Hippocrates have changed people's lives during the Hellenistic Age?

_____

_____

Lesson 1: Rome's Beginnings

A Perfect Location

According to legend, the twins Romulus and Remus founded Rome. They were the sons of a king. But the king's brother killed the king and took over. The new king tried to kill the twins. They were saved and cared for by a wolf. The twins were raised by a shepherd. Later they found out who they really were. They killed the king and founded Rome. When Romulus set up Rome, he predicted that the heavens wanted Rome to become the capital of the world. We do not know if the twins actually lived. We do know that about 1600 B.C. people came to live along the Tiber River on the Italian Peninsula. The Italian Peninsula, or Italy, is mountainous. It stretches into the Mediterranean Sea. Italy forms a kind of bridge between Western Europe, North Africa, and Western Asia. Rome is located near the middle of the western coast. The city spreads across seven low hills near the Tiber River. The hills helped protect the city from attacks and floods.

The Romans Learn from Other Cultures

In ancient times ships sailed from the Mediterranean up the Tiber River to Rome. Here they traded goods. Romans learned about growing crops from sailors who came from Greece and other faraway lands. Romans also learned stories and legends of other peoples. The Romans would continue to learn about other cultures throughout their history. The climate along the Tiber River was good for growing crops such as grapes and olives. The early peoples of Italy first called themselves Latins. They started calling themselves Romans when other villages began uniting with Rome.

Etruscan Rule

Rome grew in size. More Latins joined Rome and it became rich. The Etruscans lived north of Rome. They were powerful and took over Rome in about 600 B.C. They soon controlled almost all of the Italian Peninsula. The Etruscans may have taught the Romans about farming and building. The Romans learned how to build aqueducts, or structures that carry flowing water to cities. They also learned how to make better weapons and ships. Yet the Romans did not like Etruscan rule. Junius Brutus was a Roman leader. He helped force the Etruscans from power. Brutus became the new leader of Rome. Rome would soon enter a great period. It formed a government that people still study today.

Lesson 1: Review

1. **Main Idea and Details** Write an appropriate main idea for the three supporting details below.

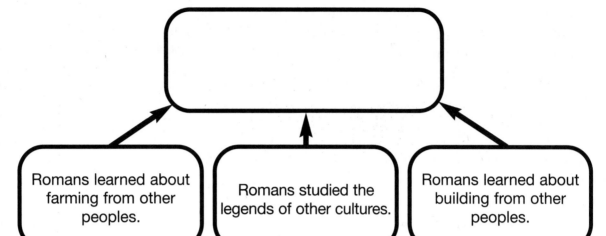

2. According to legend, who were Romulus and Remus?

_____

_____

3. Along what river was Rome built?

_____

_____

4. How did a good location help Rome grow from a small village to a powerful city?

_____

_____

5. **Critical Thinking:** *Make Inferences* What does the legend of Rome's founding tell you about how the Romans felt about their place in the world?

_____

_____

Lesson 2: The Roman Republic

Vocabulary

patrician a wealthy, powerful citizen of Rome

plebeian a Roman citizen who was not a patrician; farmers and soldiers were plebeians

republic a type of government in which citizens vote to choose their leaders

representative someone elected to represent, or speak for, the people

Senate the governing body of Rome

consul a Roman patrician who managed the government and army

dictator someone who has total control over the people

tribune a person chosen to protect the rights of the plebeians

patriotism a sense of pride in one's country

caesar a Roman ruler

The Roman Spirit

Patricians were the wealthiest, most powerful Roman citizens. **Plebeians** were all others who were not patricians. About 90 percent of Roman citizens were plebeians.

How the Romans Governed Themselves

The Romans set up a **republic.** In a republic citizens elect their leaders. Elected leaders are called **representatives.** Roman representatives served in the **Senate,** the governing body of Rome. Slaves and most foreigners were not citizens. Roman women were citizens, but could not vote or hold public office. The Senate was made up of patricians. Each year two patricians were chosen as **consuls** to run the government and army. In an emergency the consuls could name one person to rule. This **dictator** had total control over Rome.

The Tribunes

Many plebeians were very poor. The Senate named **tribunes** to protect the rights of plebeians. The tribunes became powerful. Some plebeians became wealthy. Yet the patricians still had more power than the plebeians.

Daily Life

In ancient Rome, boys and some girls from wealthy families went to school. Rich people ate meat, fish, olive oil, herbs, and dates. Poor people ate grains, bread, olives, and a little meat.

Wars with Carthage

Carthage was a powerful city-state in North Africa. Rome defeated Carthage in each of three Punic Wars. Hannibal was a Carthaginian general in the second war. He tried to invade Rome. Hannibal took his army across the Alps with a herd of elephants. Rome was saved when a general attacked Carthage. During the third war, Rome destroyed Carthage.

Problems at Home

The Romans wanted the conquered people to feel **patriotism** toward Rome. But Rome had problems. Patricians became wealthier, but many Romans became poorer. Captured slaves took jobs from the plebeians. Farms and homes were destroyed during war.

The Republic Ends

Julius Caesar was a great general and **caesar.** He won power and was made ruler for life. He was killed in 44 B.C. Civil war broke out. The Roman republic ended.

Roads in the Republic

During the republic, the Romans built concrete roads. The Appian Way is a Roman road that can still be seen today.

© Scott Foresman 6

Lesson 2: Review

1. ⟲ **Main Idea and Details** Write the appropriate details that support the main idea.

The Roman government was a republic.

Roman representatives were elected to serve in a governing body called the Senate.

2. What is a republic?

_____

_____

_____

3. Who was Hannibal and what was his greatest accomplishment?

_____

_____

_____

4. How did Rome's conquests create major problems for the republic?

_____

_____

_____

5. **Critical Thinking:** *Recognize Point of View* Do you believe the patricians shared enough power with the plebeians? Explain your answer.

_____

_____

_____

Lesson 3: The Roman Empire

Vocabulary

emperor the ruler of an empire
gladiator a professional fighter in ancient Rome

The Pax Romana

After the republic ended, Rome became an empire. **Emperors,** or rulers of an empire, governed Rome for 500 years. Augustus was the first emperor. He ruled from 27 B.C. to A.D. 14. He brought order, peace, and wealth to Rome. Life improved for most people, even for many conquered people. Augustus organized firefighters and police officers for Rome. Trade and business grew. Augustus added new land to the Empire. This period lasted for nearly 200 years. The Romans called it "the Roman Peace," or *Pax Romana* in Latin. Rome's army became the most powerful in the world. Rome controlled a huge empire on three continents.

The Good Emperors and the Bad

Caligula became emperor in A.D. 37. He was cruel and declared himself a god. He was killed by his bodyguards in A.D. 41. Claudius was the next emperor. He was a better ruler. He worked hard to improve life in the empire. Nero followed as emperor. He was as bad as Caligula. He murdered some of his family members. After his death there was civil war. In A.D. 96, Rome became peaceful again. For 84 years emperors known as the "Five Good Emperors" ruled Rome. Marcus Aurelius may have been the greatest of them.

Government and Law

The Roman Empire was huge. People spoke different languages and followed different religions. The Romans ruled them all. Many conquered people became citizens. In addition to their own languages, people across the Empire spoke Latin. They used Roman roads and were defended by Roman armies. Rome developed a code of law for everyone. These laws are the model for many nations today, including the United States.

Entertainment

Romans enjoyed watching battles in sports arenas. The Colosseum was the most famous Roman sports arena. The most popular events involved **gladiators,** or professional fighters. Most of them were prisoners or slaves. They often fought battles to the death. Crowds would watch the fights and cheer wildly.

Roman Arts

The Romans were great builders. They built sports stadiums. They built long aqueducts to bring water to cities. Cities across the Empire grew. Many people spoke Latin. Latin is the basis for many European languages spoken today, such as Spanish, Italian, French, Portuguese, and Romanian.

Lesson 3: Review

1. **Draw Conclusions** Fill in the missing details that form the conclusion.

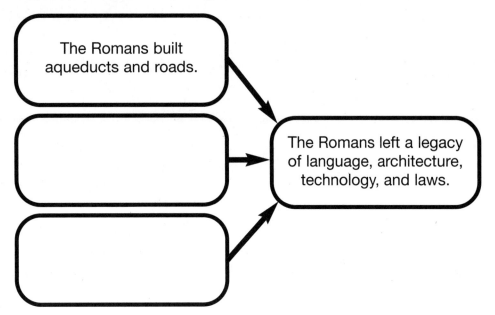

The Romans built aqueducts and roads.

The Romans left a legacy of language, architecture, technology, and laws.

2. Who was Augustus and why is he important?

_____

_____

3. What was the *Pax Romana?*

_____

_____

4. How did wise rule make the Roman Empire very powerful? Use the word **emperor** in your answer.

_____

_____

5. **Critical Thinking:** *Evaluate Information* Support the statement that Rome had an advanced civilization.

_____

_____

Lesson 4: The Rise of Christianity

Vocabulary

catacomb an underground burial room
synagogue a Jewish place of worship
disciple one of Jesus' followers
persecute to punish for one's beliefs

A New Religion

A new religion was spreading throughout the Roman Empire. It was Christianity. Christians would go into the **catacombs,** or underground burial rooms, to worship in secret. Christianity was started by Jesus. He was born in the Roman province of Palestine in present-day Jordan and Israel. His family was Jewish. Most of what we know about his life comes from four books in the part of the Bible known as the New Testament. These four books are called the Gospels. People gathered to listen to Jesus wherever he went. Sometimes he spoke in what would later become **synagogues.** They are Jewish places of worship. Twelve **disciples,** or followers, helped Jesus preach. They are called the Apostles.

What Jesus Taught

Much of what Jesus taught came from his Jewish upbringing. He taught that there was only one God. The Romans and Greeks thought that there were many gods. Jesus taught people to follow the Ten Commandments. Jesus wanted people to be kind to one another. He said that if people followed what he said and believed in God, they would go to heaven. Jesus preached about forgiveness and mercy.

Jesus' Message Spreads

Jesus' message spread across Palestine. Some local leaders thought that this would upset their Roman rulers. So the local leaders had Jesus crucified, or put to death on a cross. According to the Gospels, Jesus rose from the dead. Many people thought he was the Messiah, or the savior. A savior is someone who saves or rescues. The Apostles Peter, Paul, and others spread Jesus' teaching throughout the Mediterranean region. By A.D. 100, many people in parts of the Roman Empire were Christians.

Toward Acceptance

At first, many Christians were **persecuted,** or punished, for their beliefs. Christians refused to worship Roman emperors as gods. The religion spread. In A.D. 313, the emperor Constantine made Christianity equal to other religions. Christians were no longer allowed to be persecuted. Constantine also became a Christian. In A.D. 380, Theodosius made Christianity the main religion of Rome.

Christianity Today

Christianity is practiced all over the world. Most Christians live in Europe and the Americas. There are different Christian groups in Christianity. Each group has some different beliefs, customs, and practices. Yet Jesus is central to all Christians' beliefs. Christianity teaches that God sent his son, Jesus, into the world in human form. It teaches that Jesus was sent to help people reach salvation or eternal peace forever in God's presence when they die.

Lesson 4: Review

1. ↻ **Main Idea and Details** Write the missing detail that supports the main idea in the top box.

Christianity started in Palestine and spread throughout the Roman Empire.

Jesus was from a Jewish family in the Roman province of Palestine.

Theodosius made Christianity Rome's official religion.

2. Who were Peter and Paul and what was their major accomplishment?

_____

_____

3. Why did the Roman emperors persecute Christians?

_____

_____

4. How do you think the unity of the Roman Empire helped Christianity to become the empire's main religion?

_____

_____

_____

5. **Critical Thinking:** *Make Inferences* Review Chapter 2. How did many Christian teachings grow out of Jewish traditions?

_____

_____

_____

Lesson 5: Rise and Fall

Vocabulary

auction to sell off
pope the leader of the Roman church
pillage rob
vandal someone who destroys property

The Empire Declines

The emperor Marcus Aurelius died in A.D. 180. Most of the emperors who followed cared mostly about money and power. The Roman Empire declined, or weakened.

Emperors for Sale

In A.D. 235 the army **auctioned,** or sold off, the position of emperor to the person who paid the most for it. Then soldiers fought and put their favorites in office. Many Romans would not serve in the army. Rome had to hire soldiers called mercenaries from other lands. These mercenaries were not loyal. They did not protect Roman towns. Travel became dangerous and trade slowed.

The Empire Divides

Diocletian ruled from 284 to 305. He helped bring back order, and he made the economy stronger. Diocletian divided the huge Empire in two to govern it better. He controlled the wealthy eastern part. He named co-emperors to control the western part of the Empire. Diocletian retired as emperor in 305.

The City of Constantine

In 324 the emperor Constantine made the Empire whole again. He built a new capital city known as Constantinople. Constantinople became the center of the Byzantine Empire. After Constantine died, the "Roman" Empire split in two again. The empire in the west was weaker. Its capital was Rome. The empire in the east was stronger. Its capital was Constantinople.

Christianity Divides

In the east the emperor was the head of the Christian church. The emperor in the east chose the leaders of the church. But it was different in the west. In the west the **pope,** the leader of the Roman church, had power over all Romans including the emperor. In 1054 the churches officially divided. The Byzantine Orthodox Church was in the east. The Roman Catholic Church was in the west.

The Final Days of Rome

The Huns, a tribe from Central Asia, attacked German tribes. The German tribes fled into the Roman Empire. A German tribe called the Visigoths took over a large area in the eastern part of the Roman Empire. In 410 the Visigoth leader Alaric captured Rome. The Visigoths **pillaged,** or robbed, the city. In 455 another German tribe, the Vandals, captured and pillaged Rome. Today the word **vandal** describes someone who destroys property.

The Fall

Orestes was a powerful soldier. In 476 he had his young son, Romulus Augustulus, named emperor. A German ruler had Orestes killed. Romulus Augustulus survived. He was the last emperor of the Western Roman Empire. Constantinople became the center of Roman power. It would keep this power for another 1,000 years.

© Scott Foresman 6

Lesson 5: Review

1. Cause and Effect Fill in the missing cause and effects.

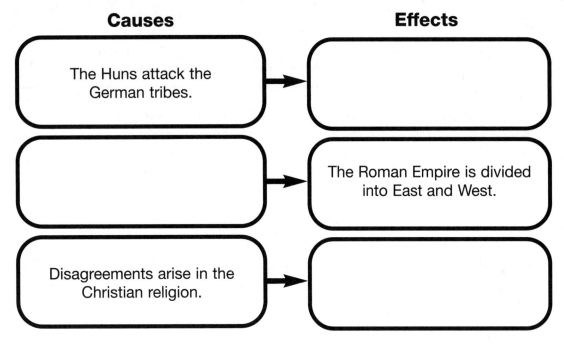

Causes **Effects**

The Huns attack the German tribes. →

→ The Roman Empire is divided into East and West.

Disagreements arise in the Christian religion. →

2. Why did the Romans hire foreign mercenaries to serve in the army?

_____

_____

3. What happened to the Roman Empire after the death of Constantine?

_____

_____

4. Why did the eastern half of the Roman Empire not suffer the same decline as the western half?

_____

_____

5. Critical Thinking: *Make Inferences* What problems do you think Rome had by having an army largely made up of mercenaries?

_____

_____

Lesson 1: Geography of the Byzantine Empire

Vocabulary

hippodrome an ancient Greek stadium used for horse and chariot racing

Roots of an Empire

The Byzantine Empire was considered a continuation of the Roman Empire. It covered areas of land that were once part of the Roman Empire. At its height, the Byzantine Empire stretched across parts of southern and eastern Europe. It also included parts of the Balkan Peninsula, northern Africa, and southwestern Asia. The summers were dry and hot in the southern and eastern parts of Europe. During the winter, the weather was wet and cool. People grew grapes, olives, wheat, and barley. Most people lived in villages. Many people herded sheep or goats. The climate in northern Africa and most of southwestern Asia was drier and hotter. The winters were warm or mild. The desert regions received little rainfall. Herders moved from place to place to feed their goats, sheep, or camels. Merchants and craftspeople lived in towns or cities. They sold and made goods.

Ultimate Location

Constantinople was the capital of the Byzantine Empire. It had a perfect location. It was on the edge of Europe and Asia. Constantinople was located on a peninsula at the southeastern end of Europe. The city sat along the strait of Bosporus. The Bosporus helps link the Black Sea and the Mediterranean Sea. Ships traveling between the Mediterranean Sea and the Black Sea had to pass through the Bosporus. This location made Constantinople an important center for trade. The city was guarded on three sides by water. For more protection, leaders built sea walls along the coasts. Constantinople was called Byzantium in ancient times. In 330 the city was renamed in honor of the Roman emperor Constantine I.

A Blend of Culture

The Byzantine Empire developed its own culture. It mixed Greek languages and Roman customs. Like the Romans, most Byzantines lived in wooden houses. As in Roman cities, the city offered public baths, steam rooms, and swimming pools. A **hippodrome** is an ancient Greek stadium that was used for horse and chariot racing. Chariot racing was a popular form of entertainment in the Byzantine Empire. Chariot races were held in the Hippodrome in Constantinople. The Hippodrome was the center of entertainment, ceremonies, and celebrations. The Byzantines called themselves Romans. Yet they mostly spoke the Greek language. Constantinople became the main center of art, architecture, and education. The city's location helped bring about a blend of European and Asian cultures. The Byzantine Empire began to become strong after the western part of the Roman Empire became weak.

Lesson 1: Review

1. ⟳ **Sequence** The following events are not in chronological order. List them in their correct time order.

    _____ A city is established at the strait of Bosporus.

    _____ The Roman Empire weakens.

    _____ Constantinople is fortified with sea and land walls.

2. Describe how the physical geography and climate of the Byzantine Empire affected the way people lived.

    _____

    _____

    _____

    _____

3. What city was the capital of the Byzantine Empire?

    _____

    _____

    _____

    _____

4. How was the Byzantine Empire related to the Roman Empire?

    _____

    _____

    _____

    _____

5. **Critical Thinking:** *Make Inferences* Why did Constantinople become a center of trade?

    _____

    _____

    _____

    _____

© Scott Foresman 6

Lesson 2: The Greatness of the Byzantine Empire

Vocabulary

cathedral a large important Christian church
icon a picture or an image of Jesus and the saints

Byzantine Glory

In 527 Justinian became the emperor of the Byzantine Empire. He wanted to rebuild the Roman Empire and rule it as a whole. In order to do this, he paid the Persians to stop attacking western Asia. He also expanded the Empire. He took over North Africa, Italy, part of Spain, and some islands in the Mediterranean Sea. Theodora was Justinian's wife and political advisor. When Constantinople was attacked in 532, Theodora told Justinian to stay and defend the city. The Byzantine Empire was at its greatest during Justinian's rule. He rebuilt the magnificent Hagia Sophia in Constantinople. The Hagia Sophia was a **cathedral,** or a large important Christian church. Justinian also helped bring about the Justinian Code. The Justinian Code was based on Roman laws. This code organized the Roman laws and made them more clear. The Justinian Code helped the Empire's government to run fairly and smoothly.

The Glorious Church

Under Justinian's rule many new harbors, aqueducts, and buildings were built. Many cathedrals also were built. The greatest cathedral in the empire was the Hagia Sophia. Byzantine emperors and the church had close ties. The Byzantine, or Eastern, Orthodox Church was the main church. It ran political and cultural life. Justinian believed that he was chosen by God to run the Empire. The church also believed this and protected him. In about 1000 the Empire weakened. In 1054 the Christian church split in two. One reason it split was because Christians disagreed over how religious icons should be used. A religious **icon** is a picture or an image of Jesus and the saints. The Roman Catholic Church and the Byzantine Orthodox Church were two separate churches after 1054.

Lesson 2: Review

1. ⟳ **Sequence** The following events are not in the correct order. List them in their correct chronological order.

   _____ The Hagia Sophia was built in Constantinople.

   _____ Justinian added Italy to the Byzantine Empire.

   _____ Theodora encouraged Justinian to defend Constantinople.

2. What was the significance of the Hagia Sophia to the Byzantine Empire?

   _____

   _____

   _____

   _____

3. Who were Justinian and Theodora?

   _____

   _____

   _____

   _____

4. What are icons and what were their significance in the Byzantine Orthodox Church?

   _____

   _____

   _____

5. **Critical Thinking:** *Fact or Opinion* Justinian built the Hagia Sophia to keep close ties with the Christian church.

   _____

   _____

   _____

   _____

© Scott Foresman 6

Lesson 3: Development of Islam

Vocabulary

pilgrimage a journey to a place of religious importance
caravan a group of people and animals traveling together
mosque a Muslim place of worship

Birth of Islam

Muhammad was born in Mecca about 570. For some time Muhammad lived with a desert tribe and tended sheep and camels. He traveled on caravan journeys through Arabia. **Caravans** are groups of people and animals traveling together. At this time, most people in the area worshipped many gods. They prayed to spirits and idols, or objects used in worship. This troubled Muhammad. Muhammad went to the desert to pray and meditate. According to Islamic belief, in 610 an angel came to Muhammad while he was meditating. The angel said, "Arise and warn, magnify thy Lord . . . wait patiently for Him." According to the Quran, the holy book of Islam, Muhammad had more visions. By about 613 Muhammad began to preach in public. He taught that there is only one God and this God wants people to submit to, or obey, him. The Arabic word for submission is *Islam*. Islam became the name of the religion. Muslims are the followers of Islam. They believe that God spoke directly to Muhammad. The pilgrimage, or hajj, to Mecca is an essential part of Islam. A **pilgrimage** is a journey to a place of religious importance.

The Message of Islam

After 622 Islam spread quickly across Southwest Asia. Muhammad died in 632. Islam kept spreading. People all over the world became Muslims. All Muslims follow five basic duties. These duties are called the "Pillars of Islam." First pillar: "There is no god but God and Muhammad is his prophet." Muslims believe that God sent many prophets, or great spiritual teachers. These prophets include Abraham, Moses, and Jesus. But

Muhammad was the last and the most important prophet. Second pillar: Muslims pray five times a day. Prayers are offered in a **mosque,** or a Muslim place of worship. Third pillar: Muslims must give charity to the poor. Fourth pillar: Muslims fast during the ninth month of the Muslim calendar, Ramadan. They may not eat during the day. Fifth pillar: Muslims must make at least one pilgrimage to Mecca—if at all possible.

Way of Life

Most Muslims follow certain practices in their everyday lives. The jihad is a part of Islam. *Jihad* means "struggle." Jihad can mean both military and peaceful struggles. For example, Muslims can struggle, or work hard, to better their communities. The Quran tells Muslims how to live their daily lives. It tells them what not to eat and drink, such as pork and alcohol. The Quran contains information on how to deal with marriage, divorce, and business. Muslims worship in mosques on Friday afternoons. Islam does not have a central religious leader. It has religious teachers who study the Quran and the acts of Muhammad.

Quick Study

Lesson 3: Review

1. **Main Idea and Details** Fill in the missing detail that describes Islam.

```
                    ┌────────────────────────────┐
                    │                            │
                    │  Islam is a major world    │
                    │       religion.            │
                    │                            │
                    └────────────────────────────┘
          ↗                    ↑                    ↖
┌──────────────────┐  ┌──────────────────┐  ┌──────────────────┐
│                  │  │                  │  │                  │
│ Taught by the    │  │                  │  │ Teaches Five     │
│ prophet          │  │                  │  │ Pillars          │
│ Muhammad         │  │                  │  │                  │
└──────────────────┘  └──────────────────┘  └──────────────────┘
```

2. What is the relationship between Muhammad and Islam?

_____

_____

_____

3. What is the Quran?

_____

_____

_____

4. What changes did Islam bring to Southwest Asia?

_____

_____

_____

5. **Critical Thinking:** *Make Inferences* Why might a Muslim look at the Quran when faced with a business decision?

_____

_____

_____

Lesson 4: The Islamic World

Vocabulary

astrolabe a tool used to determine latitude

Islamic Culture Spreads

Muhammad wanted Islam to spread beyond the Arabian Peninsula to many parts of the world. Islam spread through trade and war. Between the seventh and tenth centuries, Muslims took over many lands outside of the Arabian Peninsula. By 1453 Muslim soldiers had conquered Constantinople. It became the capital of their empire, the Ottoman Empire. Muslims took over much of what was once the Byzantine Empire. Muslim traders brought Islam to Southeast Asia, Central Asia, China, North Africa, and sub-Saharan Africa. Islam brought with it a system of government, laws, and society. The Quran was to be written only in Arabic. Therefore, the Arabic language spread along with Islam. Non-Muslims were treated differently than Muslims. They had to pay a special tax. They could not marry Muslim women. Their houses and churches or synagogues could not be out in the open. They could not hold positions of power. By the end of the tenth century, Islamic culture was known in many parts of the world.

Trading Ideas

Trade and conquest helped different cultures share ideas, the arts, and technology. Ibn Battuta was a Muslim traveler and historian. He learned about different peoples and lands. He traded goods and ideas from many cultures across the Islamic world. The Muslims were the first people to use branch-banking. Several banks were set up in different parts of the Muslim world. These banks worked together as one bank. People could cash checks at any of these banks. This saved time and made trade safer. People did not have to carry gold and silver that could be stolen. Muslim engineers built irrigation systems. Muslim

scientists made discoveries in chemistry. Muslims did much work in mathematics. A Muslim developed algebra. Mathematics had many uses in Islamic culture. People used it to figure out distances. They also used it to figure out the times of day to call Muslims to prayer. Muslim scientists used the astrolabe to look at the position of stars. An **astrolabe** is a tool used by astronomers to determine directions. Then they could make accurate maps for navigators. Muslim scientists also developed a calendar. Calendars and maps helped Muslims know when to make pilgrimages to Mecca and how to get there. Muslims also made advancements in medicine.

Experts at Sea

Trade grew in the Islamic world. Muslim sailors were expert navigators. They used many kinds of tools. The astrolabe helped sailors find their position at sea. Muslim sailors made ships with triangular sails that could sail into the wind as well as with the wind. These tools helped sailors reach other lands and spread Islamic culture.

© Scott Foresman 6

Lesson 4: Review

1. **Cause and Effect** Fill in an effect for each of the following causes.

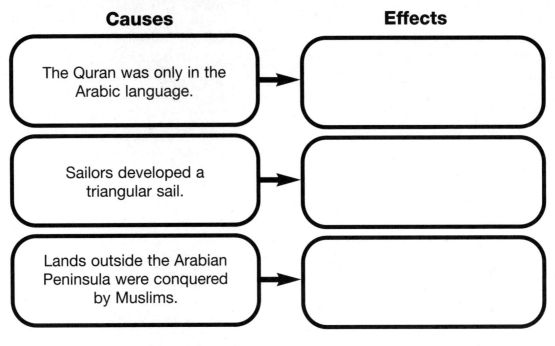

Causes   **Effects**

The Quran was only in the Arabic language.

Sailors developed a triangular sail.

Lands outside the Arabian Peninsula were conquered by Muslims.

2. How did Islam spread beyond the Arabian Peninsula?

_____

_____

3. In the Islamic world, how were non-Muslims treated differently?

_____

_____

4. What united the lands in the Islamic world?

_____

_____

5. **Critical Thinking:** *Make Generalizations* How did the knowledge of the oceans and the development of technology in navigation help expand the Islamic world? Use the word **astrolabe** in your answer.

_____

_____

Lesson 1: Empires of Asia

Asia

Asia is the largest continent on Earth. The Arctic Ocean lies to the north. The Pacific Ocean lies to the east. The Indian Ocean lies to the south. To the west are Europe, the Black Sea, the Greek Islands, the Mediterranean Sea, and the Red Sea. Asia has many types of physical features. There are huge areas of flat lands. Asia also has the world's tallest mountains. Asia has many types of climates. Northern parts are snowy all year. Tropical rain forests are found in Southeast Asia. Central Asia has many mountains. Melted snow from the mountains keeps Asia's rivers full of water. Over time people moved from the dry areas in Central and southwestern Asia to South and Southeast Asia. They also moved there from the Arabian Peninsula. Mountain ranges protected people in Korea, Japan, and China from other peoples. Today most Asians live in river or mountain valleys. Other Asians live near seacoasts where they fish or farm. Agriculture is Asia's main economic activity.

The Mogul Empire

Different groups of people invaded India from 455 to the early 1500s. Babur was a leader from Central Asia. In 1526 he took over parts of northern India. This began the Mogul Empire. Babur then took over much of northern India. Akbar was Babur's grandson. He became the greatest Mogul emperor. Akbar ruled from 1556 to 1605. He conquered most of India. Akbar wanted to keep his empire united. In order to do this, he tried to win the support of non-Muslims in the empire. He changed and strengthened the central government. Akbar collected taxes in an unusual way. Every member of the empire, including nobles and peasants, had to pay land tax. The tax depended on the value of the crops grown on the land. Past rulers had only taxed crops of farmers.

From Rise to Fall

Most people in India were Hindus. The Mogul emperors were Muslims. Under Emperor Akbar, some Hindus served as Mogul generals and governors. Others were officers and clerks. The Hindus and the Muslims lived together peacefully. The Mogul Empire soon became very rich and powerful. Shah Jahan was Akbar's grandson. He ruled the Mogul Empire from 1628 to 1658. He ordered builders to construct the Taj Mahal, the greatest building in India. The Taj Mahal was built to honor the memory of Shah Jahan's wife. Aurangzeb was Shah Jahan's son. Aurangzeb was a harsh ruler. He treated Hindus and other non-Muslims badly. He tried to make them change their religion to Islam. The people of western and southern India rebelled. The Mogul Empire began to fall apart.

© Scott Foresman 6

Lesson 1: Review

1. **Sequence** List the following events in the correct chronological order.

_____ Mogul forces control much of northern India.

_____ The Mogul Empire crumbles.

_____ Babur establishes Mogul Empire.

_____ Akbar rules much of India.

2. Why is there a variety of cultures in Asia?

_____

_____

_____

_____

3. Who was the first Mogul ruler of India?

_____

_____

_____

_____

4. What was unusual about Akbar's tax policy?

_____

_____

_____

_____

5. **Critical Thinking:** *Make Inferences* How would cooperation between the Hindus and Muslims help build a rich and powerful Empire?

_____

_____

_____

_____

© Scott Foresman 6

Lesson 2: Chinese Dynasties

Sui, Tang, and Song Dynasties

China had almost 400 years of unrest. Then the Sui dynasty united China in 589. The Sui set up a canal system. Later these canals carried water throughout China. The Tang dynasty followed. It was one of China's greatest dynasties. Empress Wu Hou was part of this dynasty. She was China's first female ruler. Under Wu Hou's rule, government workers had to pass a civil service examination. The invention of block printing let people reprint pages. Paper money was printed. Trade grew and China had more contact with different Asian cultures. After the Tang dynasty lost power, China had 50 years of war and dishonest leaders. In 960 the Song dynasty reunited China. It established a central government. Trade was very important to China's economy at this time. People discovered how to make iron in a better way. Farm workers used the iron plow to produce more crops. Iron was also used to build bridges and armor for soldiers. Soldiers first used gunpowder during Song rule.

Mongol and Ming Dynasties

Genghis Khan was a warrior. In 1206 he united nomadic, or wandering, groups from northern Asia. This formed a unified Mongolia. Genghis Khan was named ruler. He used terror to expand his empire. Genghis Khan formed a fierce army. This army defeated the people of northern China and Persia. Genghis Khan died in 1227. His sons expanded the empire. Kublai Khan was the grandson of Genghis Khan. He conquered southern China and Burma by 1280. This began the Mongol, or Yuan, dynasty. Kublai Khan was the first non-Chinese ruler of China. The Mongols improved the lands they conquered. They improved roads and water travel. They made sure that traders could travel safely. They knew that trade brought wealth to the empire. By 1368 the Ming dynasty came into power. Under Ming rule there were great achievements in the sciences and arts. Ming emperors wanted better protection against invaders. They strengthened the Great Wall. The Forbidden City was the name of the emperor's palace. It was built between 1406 and 1421. It was located in Beijing. The Forbidden City was made up of hundreds of buildings surrounded by high walls. Only the highest government officials could enter. During the Ming dynasty, Chinese people believed that their culture was the greatest in the world.

China Explores

The Ming Dynasty was a time of exploration. Zheng He was a Chinese explorer during the Ming dynasty. He led several expeditions to Southeast and Southwest Asia, India, and Africa. The Ming emperor supported the expeditions. He filled the ships with riches. The emperor told Zheng He to give them as gifts to the people he met on his voyages. The emperor wanted foreigners to see China as wealthy and powerful. He also hoped that other countries would send representatives to China. Some countries did send representatives to China. However the emperor died. The expeditions stopped by 1433. Under a new emperor, China soon cut itself off from the rest of the world. Foreigners were no longer welcome in China.

Lesson 2: Review

1. **Main Idea and Details** Fill in the missing details below.

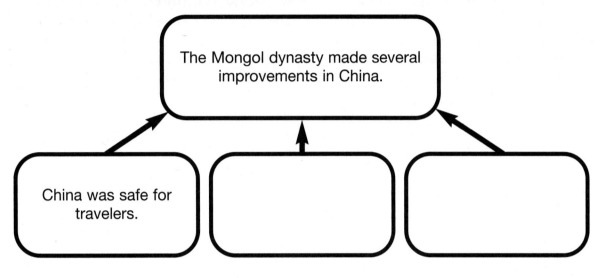

2. Identify some of the contributions made by Chinese dynasties.

_____

_____

_____

3. Where and what is the Forbidden City?

_____

_____

_____

4. What was the purpose behind Zheng He's expeditions abroad?

_____

_____

_____

5. **Critical Thinking:** *Make Inferences* What benefits might government officials have if positions in China were based on examination results, rather than family ties?

_____

_____

_____

Lesson 3: The Khmer

The Khmer Kingdom

The Khmer was one of the richest kingdoms in Southeast Asia. In the sixth century, the Khmer ruled the present-day countries of Cambodia and Laos. The Khmer culture was influenced by Indian culture. In the eighth century, fighting divided the kingdom. In 802 Jayavarman II reunited the kingdom. He was declared a deva-raja, or god-king. He was made king according to Hindu tradition. All deva-raja rulers could act with absolute power. They controlled every part of society. The Khmer rulers formed large armies. These armies defended the kingdom. They also invaded other kingdoms. Khmer kings forced their people and slaves to build a special irrigation system. The irrigation system was very important to the Khmer economy. The irrigation system kept farmland from being flooded during times of heavy rain. In addition, the irrigation system stored water. This water could be used during dry seasons. The irrigation system allowed farmers to grow crops up to two or three times a year. Surplus crops helped the economy stay strong. The kingdom influenced Southeast Asia for more than 500 years. The first royal city was built in Angkor in the tenth century. The empire was at its peak in the early twelfth century. Suryavarman II ruled from 1113 to 1150. The great towers of Angkor Wat were built during his rule.

A Stone Wonder

Over time the Khmer became great artists and builders. Their early buildings and temples were simple. Later their temples became more complex. By the end of the Khmer rule, there were more than 70 great temples and monuments in Angkor. Many temple walls were decorated with scenes from everyday life or battles. The temple of Angkor Wat is the finest Khmer building. Angkor Wat was built to honor to the Hindu god Vishnu. The temple also became the tomb of the Khmer king who had it built. It took 50,000 people and nearly 40 years to complete Angkor Wat.

Lesson 3: Review

1. **Cause and Effect** Fill in one cause or effect for each blank.

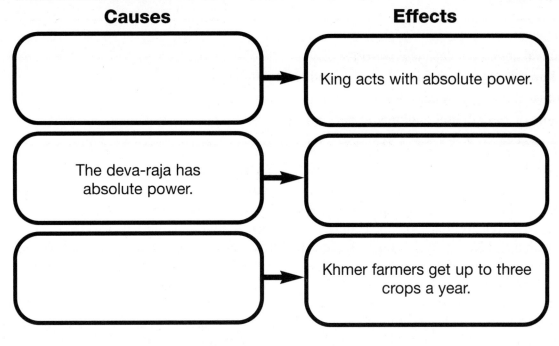

Causes   **Effects**

	King acts with absolute power.
The deva-raja has absolute power.	
	Khmer farmers get up to three crops a year.

2. Where was the first royal city located?

   _____

   _____

3. What role did irrigation play in the Khmer economy?

   _____

   _____

4. Why were the Khmer able to dominate Southeast Asia for centuries?

   _____

   _____

5. **Critical Thinking:** *Make Generalizations* Why do you think the Khmer were willing to devote so much time and energy to constructing the temple complex?

   _____

   _____

Lesson 4: Japan in Isolation

Vocabulary

aristocrat a noble
samurai a class of Japanese warriors
typhoon a tropical storm with heavy winds and rough seas
daimyo a ruling samurai leader
shogun a special, high-ranking military office

Early Japan

Early Japan was made up of 100 states. By the early 600s these states united. The country had its first constitution. Japan had contact with China and Korea. This brought Buddhism and the Chinese system of writing to Japan. Noble families soon had important positions in the government. They worked to weaken the emperor's power. They set up private estates, or areas of land that the emperor had no control over. The government and the **aristocrats,** or nobles, began to depend on the samurai for protection. The **samurai** were a class of warriors. They protected the land of the aristocrats and kept society in order. In 1192 the samurai took away the emperor's ruling power. In the late 1200s, Mongols from China tried to conquer Japan. **Typhoons,** or tropical storms, helped Japan stop the Mongols. The Japanese began to believe that they were special. During the 1500s the daimyo fought each other for land and power. The **daimyo** were powerful samurai leaders in Japan. Fighting among daimyo led to a civil war. Toyotomi Hideyoshi was a Japanese general. In 1590 he brought together several groups that were fighting. He controlled most of Japan until he died. Tokugawa Ieyasu was a daimyo. He took power and established the Tokugawa dynasty.

Tokugawa Rule

In 1603 the emperor of Japan gave Tokugawa Ieyasu the title of shogun. A **shogun** is a special, high-ranking military office. The Tokugawa dynasty shoguns would rule Japan for 265 years. Shoguns controlled foreign trade. They ran gold and silver mines. They ruled over major cities such as Edo. Edo was the shogun capital. Shoguns shared power with the daimyo. Shoguns controlled 25 percent of Japan's farmland. Daimyo controlled the rest. The daimyo made laws and collected taxes. The social system had four classes. The samurai made up the ruling class. Merchants, artisans, and farmers made up the other classes. The division among classes was important to the Tokugawa shoguns. They used different groups of daimyo against each other. Because shoguns controlled foreign trade, the daimyo could not become too wealthy or powerful. Soon Japan began following a policy of isolation. This meant that Japan had very little contact with other cultures. Most foreigners were forced to leave the country. Japanese people could not travel to other countries. Most foreign books were banned. Japan traded only with China, Korea, and the Netherlands. This was because shoguns wanted to keep some contact with the outside world. Japan's trade grew during this time. The shogun government began to owe a lot of money. The merchant class became wealthier and more powerful. Farmers were charged higher taxes. The farmers rebelled against these taxes. The class system began to fall apart.

© Scott Foresman 6

Lesson 4: Review

1. Cause and Effect Fill in the missing cause or effect.

Causes	Effects

The shogun controls all foreign trade. →

Japan follows a policy of isolation. →

→ Farmers riot.

2. Which Japanese city was the shogun's capital during the Tokugawa dynasty?

_____

_____

3. What is the difference between a samurai and a shogun?

_____

_____

4. How did Japan's policy of isolation affect Japanese trade and culture?

_____

_____

5. Critical Thinking: *Make Inferences* Why did shoguns allow some trade with other countries?

_____

_____

Lesson 1: The Geography of Africa

Vocabulary

savanna short grassy plains

Climate Zones

Africa is the second largest continent on Earth. It has eight climate zones. Some of these zones are desert, savanna, rain forest, and Mediterranean. The desert zone is hot and dry. It includes the Sahara, the largest desert in the world. Very few plants and animals are found in the desert. The **savanna,** or grassy plains, covers about half of Africa. Here the ground is good for growing crops or herding cattle. There is only a small area of rain forests in Africa. It is almost impossible to farm there because of the thick plant life. The Mediterranean climate is mild. Summers are hot and winters are mild and rainy. Some areas have fertile land that is good for farming.

Mountains and Rivers

The climate in Africa affects how people and goods can move. Traders in the desert face sandstorms and heat. They find little water. Also, different African landforms can slow journeys. These landforms include mountains, plateaus, cataracts, and valleys. The Great Rift Valley is in East Africa. It is so big it can be seen from space. Plateaus cover much of the central part of Africa. Many rivers flow from the plateaus to the coast. The main rivers include the Zambezi, Congo, Niger, and Nile. Many people used these rivers to move trade goods.

Spread of Peoples

Changes in climate caused people to move around Africa. The Sahara was once wet and had grasses and trees. The climate changed and little rain fell. People then left the area. People also moved because resources had been used up. Linguists were able to trace the movements of some of these people. Linguists are people who study languages. They noticed that a language group called Bantu is spoken in many parts of Africa today. Many words in the Bantu languages are similar. Linguists believe that a group that spoke Bantu traveled south in Africa between 100 B.C. and A.D. 1500. They spread their languages as they moved across Africa.

Lesson 1: Review

1. **Summarize** Write three short sentences to form the summary below.

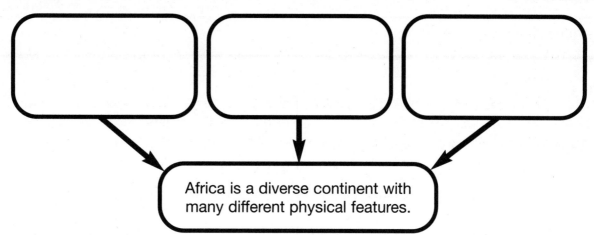

Africa is a diverse continent with many different physical features.

2. Describe the major climate zones of Africa.

_____

_____

_____

3. What are the major rivers of Africa?

_____

_____

_____

4. How did Africans adapt to their environment?

_____

_____

_____

5. **Critical Thinking:** *Make Generalizations* Why do linguists believe that the Bantu speakers spread across Africa?

_____

_____

_____

Lesson 2: West African Kingdoms

Vocabulary

griot a professional storyteller

Ghana

Gold was valuable in West Africa. The ancient kingdom of Ghana was known for its gold trade. Ghana was founded in about A.D. 300 by the Soninke people. It is believed that people in Ghana farmed, fished, and herded cattle. Ghana was located between salt mines in the Sahara and gold fields in Wangara. Ghana became a great trading empire by the late 900s. Berber people from North Africa helped traders get across the Sahara. The Berbers helped keep thieves away from the trade routes. Safe routes kept Ghana's capital, Koumbi, a major trade center. Ghana taxed major trade items. This made the empire even richer. Muslim traders brought new ideas and the religion of Islam to Ghana. By the early 1000s, the Soninke people began to lose control of Ghana. Different groups fought for power. By 1203 King Sumanguru took control of the empire.

Mali

In 1235 Sundiata defeated King Sumanguru. Sundiata started the empire of Mali. Sundiata's life story is still told by **griots,** or professional storytellers. People in Mali grew rice, onions, grains, yams, and cotton. Mali depended on trade for wealth. Gold was discovered in the empire. This made Mali wealthy. By 1300 Mali was the most powerful empire in Africa. Mansa Musa, Sundiata's grandson, became a great king. He was a Muslim. Mansa Musa is known for his trip to Mecca. On this trip he took thousands of people, gold, camels, and other supplies. He stopped in Egypt along the way. Many Egyptian writers remembered his wealth, intelligence, and generosity. Mansa Musa brought back an Arab architect to build mosques in Timbuktu, a trading city in Mali. He also brought back Arab scholars to teach Muslim beliefs. His trip to Mecca interested European mapmakers. Europeans also became interested in Mali's resources.

Jenne-jenno

Jenne-jenno was a city on the Niger River. It was the oldest known city in sub-Saharan Africa. People first settled there about 200 B.C. During the Mali empire, trade goods were brought to Jenne-jenno. The goods were shipped on the river to Timbuktu. By 1400 the city was deserted. No one is certain why.

Songhai

The Songhai were farmers, traders, and warriors. They had fought to stay independent of Mali. By about 1464 the Songhai empire began taking over the land around it. King Sonni Ali helped make Songhai an even bigger trade and learning center than Mali had been. He split the empire into different states. Governors ruled these states. The king created an army and navy to protect his kingdom and trade. Yet the empire did not last as long as those of Ghana and Mali. Fighting among different Muslim groups led some states to leave the empire. In 1591 the Songhai empire was attacked by the Moroccans. They defeated the Songhai using a new technology, guns.

Lesson 2: Review

1. **Summarize** Write a summary of the sentences listed below.

| Trade made Ghana a wealthy empire. | Mali traded with its great quantities of gold. | Songhai became a great center of trade in West Africa. |

2. What was the role of Ghana in the movement of trade goods across the Sahara?

_____

_____

3. Who was Mansa Musa?

_____

_____

4. How were the West African kingdoms crossroads for trade?

_____

_____

_____

5. **Critical Thinking: *Make Inferences*** Why would European mapmakers include Mali on their maps after hearing about Mansa Musa's pilgrimage to Mecca?

_____

_____

Lesson 3: East, Central, and Southern Africa

Vocabulary

Swahili a combination of African and Arabic cultures and languages
oba a king in Benin

East Africa

Meroë was a trade center in East Africa. In about 350 Meroë was invaded by the kingdom of Axum. Axum was in the Ethiopian highlands. Axum traded ivory, frankincense, and myrrh with Greece and Rome. It also traded items made from brass, copper, and glass crystal. In return, Axum received cloth, jewelry, metals, and steel. Axum and other kingdoms in northeastern Africa were Christian. In the seventh century, Arabs invaded Egypt. The invasions did not destroy Axum. Changing climate and moving trade routes forced people to abandon Axum.

Ethiopia

Ethiopia replaced the Axum civilization. The Zagwe dynasty took over in about 1150. The Zagwe established Christianity in Ethiopia. They moved the capital to Adefa. Between 1185 and 1225, 11 great stone churches were built at Adefa. In 1270 the Solomonid dynasty took over the Zagwe dynasty. It ruled until 1974. Solomonid rulers stopped building great churches and palaces. There was no longer a permanent capital. The king and court moved up to three times a year.

Kilwa

Indian Ocean trade began in northern cities along the eastern coast of Africa. By the ninth century, southern cities such as Kilwa began trading gold and ivory. The Indian Ocean trade network ran from East Africa to India, China, and Arabia. Some Arabs settled along the coast of East Africa. East African and Muslim cultures mixed. This mixture formed the **Swahili** language and culture. In the 1500s the Portuguese invaded Kilwa and other coastal cities. Swahili groups later regained control of many ports along the coast.

Great Zimbabwe

The city of Great Zimbabwe was named for the stone walls built around it. Great Zimbabwe was part of the gold and ivory trade. It made a lot of money by taxing gold. People left Great Zimbabwe in about 1450. They had used up all of their resources. The Portuguese invaded the area and took over the kingdom in the late 1600s.

Benin

The kingdom of Benin was near the delta of the Niger River. Its people lived in a forest region. Benin's kings were called **obas.** They came into power around 1300. Portuguese traders began trading coral beads and cloth for Benin's ivory, animal skins, and pepper. Benin became a powerful empire by 1500. It was trading cloth, spices, and slaves. Large walls were built to guard the kingdom's wealth. The people in Benin farmed. People lived in both the capital city and the country. Houses were made of mud. Benin was known for sculptures and carvings made of bronze, ivory, and wood.

© Scott Foresman 6

Name _____ Date _____

Lesson 3: Review

1. Summarize Fill in the missing detail to complete the summary below.

Axum was abandoned after Arab invasions.		Ethiopia took over the position of the old kingdom of Axum.

Axum replaced Meroë in A.D. 350. Later, Ethiopia took over the old kingdom of Axum after it was invaded and abandoned.

2. List goods that were traded in eastern, central, and southern Africa.

_____

_____

3. How were the civilizations that existed in eastern, central, and southern Africa alike and different?

_____

_____

4. How were these civilizations influenced by other civilizations in the Indian Ocean trade network? Use the word **Swahili** in your answer.

_____

_____

5. Critical Thinking: *Make Inferences* What might life have been like in these regions if they had not participated in international trade? Explain your answer.

_____

_____

Lesson 1: Geography of Europe

Europe

Europe is the second smallest continent on Earth. It stretches from the Arctic Ocean in the north to the Mediterranean Sea in the south. The Atlantic Ocean is to the west. The Ural Mountains lie to the east. These mountains separate Europe from Asia. Europe has four main land regions: the Northwest Mountains, the North European Plain, the Central Uplands, and the Alpine Mountain System. The Northwest Mountains area is not good for farming. It has steep slopes and thin soil. The North European Plain is part of the Great European Plain, which covers much of Europe. Its flat and rolling land is very good for farming. The Central Uplands has mountains, plateaus, and forests. Some of its land is rocky and some is used for farming. The Alpine Mountain System has several mountain chains. These include the Alps and the Carpathian Mountains. The valleys and lower slopes in the region are good for farming. Its higher slopes are covered with forests. Above the timberline are meadows. They are used as pastureland.

Europe's River System

Europe has many rivers. They are used as transportation routes. These include the Volga River, the Danube River, and the Rhine River. Europe's weather is milder than parts of Asia and North America at the same latitude. This is because the Gulf Stream warms the winds in Europe. The Gulf Stream is a strong ocean current. It carries warm water from the Gulf of Mexico to the western coast of Europe. For thousands of years, traders have moved goods along Europe's waterways. Many cities grew near rivers. People began to fish in the North Atlantic. This made fishing an important part of Europe's economy.

Climate and Landforms

In the Middle Ages, Europeans began clearing land to farm. Climate and landforms affected which crops they farmed and where they planted them. The Northern European Plain has good farmland. Wheat and other grains are grown there. Most of Europe has a mild climate. But different areas do have different climates. The Atlantic coast has mild winters and cool summers. This climate is good for farming. Southern Europe has hot and dry summers. Its winters are mild and rainy. People farmed in this area too much. The soil is no longer as good as it once was for growing crops. In the Northwest Mountain region, the climate changes according to the elevation. At lower spots, people can farm because the climate is mild. Many people also herd animals and cut timber in these areas.

Lesson 1: Review

1. 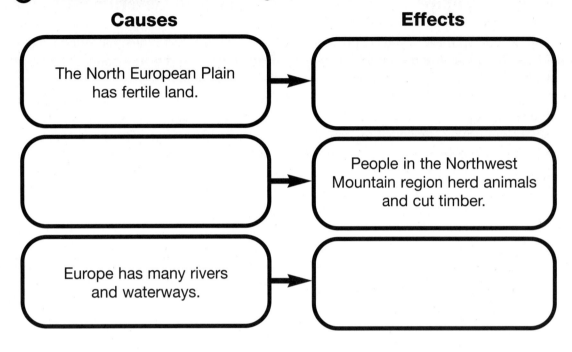 **Cause and Effect** Fill in the missing cause and effects.

Causes		Effects
The North European Plain has fertile land.	→	
	→	People in the Northwest Mountain region herd animals and cut timber.
Europe has many rivers and waterways.	→	

2. What major landform separates Europe from Asia?

_____

_____

3. What are the major rivers of Europe?

_____

_____

4. Identify some ways in which Europeans modified their landscape.

_____

_____

5. **Critical Thinking:** *Accuracy of Information* If you read in a book that Europe had climate regions that were mostly dry and hot, would that be correct? Explain.

_____

_____

Lesson 2: Rulers and Invaders

A European Empire

The Domesday Book was put together in 1086. It helped keep track of how many people lived in England in the Middle Ages. The Middle Ages is the time in Europe from A.D. 500 to 1500. The Domesday Book also helped to set up a tax system. Before the Domesday Book, rulers depended on records kept by nobles. Charlemagne was a European ruler. In 800 Pope Leo III named Charlemagne emperor of the former Roman Empire in western Europe. Charlemagne wanted nobles to be loyal to him. Therefore, he gave them a lot of land.

Invaders

After Charlemagne's death, his kingdom fell apart. From about 800 to 1100, Vikings invaded. Vikings were warriors from Scandinavia. They raided parts of England, France, Germany, Ireland, Russia, and Spain. Later the Vikings set up trading centers and trade routes in these places. In the early 900s, the Normans settled in northern France. The Normans were another Viking group. They became Christians and church leaders. Led by William the Conqueror, they invaded England and southern Italy.

A Change in Government

English kings had the power to do whatever they wanted. Most kings that ruled from 1066 through the 1100s were strong and just. In 1199 King John took power. He ruled in a way that made people angry. For example, he sold royal jobs to those who paid the highest prices. In 1214 King John lost a battle against France. A civil war began in England. John wanted to end the fight against him. He agreed to sign the Magna Carta in 1215. This document limited royal power. It said that kings could not ask for money without the agreement of the lords. It also said that free people could be punished only if they broke the law. The Magna Carta made sure that the king also followed the law.

Lesson 2: Review

1. ⟳ **Sequence** Put these events in their correct chronological order.

_____ King John signs the Magna Carta.

_____ Charlemagne is crowned emperor.

_____ William the Conqueror invades England.

_____ The Vikings invade Europe.

2. What title did Pope Leo III give Charlemagne?

_____

_____

_____

_____

3. How did the Domesday Book help kings rule their kingdoms?

_____

_____

_____

_____

4. How did the Magna Carta limit royal power?

_____

_____

_____

_____

5. **Critical Thinking:** *Fact or Opinion* The Magna Carta indicated that there should be no taxation without the consent of the lords.

_____

_____

_____

_____

Lesson 3: Life in the Middle Ages

Vocabulary

monk a man who devotes his life to religion

nun a woman who devotes her life to religion

monastery a place where monks study, pray, and live

convent a place where nuns study, pray, and live

missionary a person who teaches a religion to people with different beliefs

monarch a king or queen

serf a peasant in the Middle Ages; serfs lived on the land and farmed it

knight a warrior trained to fight on horseback

chivalry a code of behavior for knights

guild a group of people united by a common interest

lady a noblewoman

The Church

In the Middle Ages, most Europeans were Christians. Some were Jews or Muslims. The Christian leader, the pope, lived in Rome. **Monks** were men who devoted their lives to religion. Monks lived in **monasteries. Nuns** were women who devoted their lives to Christianity. They lived in **convents.** Some monks were **missionaries.** They taught Christianity to people of other religions.

Feudalism

Feudalism was a political, social, and economic system that began in the 800s. It had four levels: monarchs, lords, knights, and serfs. The **monarch** was the main ruler. The lords received land for their loyalty. Lords got money from crops grown on the land. Lords kept order and collected taxes. **Serfs** farmed the land. Many lords had **knights.** Knights followed a code of behavior called **chivalry.**

Feudalism Declines

Serfs were at the bottom of feudal society. They were not slaves. They were tied to the land and could not leave it without their lord's permission. Some lords built up military power and became independent. Feudalism began to crumble by the 1400s.

The Manor System

Most manors had four parts: the manor house and village, farmland, meadowland, and wasteland. The lord lived in the manor house. Serfs lived in the village. Life as a serf was hard. Serfs farmed using the three-field rotation system. Under this system every serf worked three pieces of land in each of the manor's three fields. Serfs sold extra crops to people in towns and cities. This food helped towns and cities grow.

Guilds

A **guild** was a group of people who worked together to reach a common goal. Merchant guilds were started by traders. These guilds bought large amounts of goods cheaply. People who were not members of guilds could not sell their goods in town. Craft guilds were formed by workers such as bakers, tailors, and weavers. Craft guilds made sure crafts were made well. They also controlled how many of an item could be made.

Medieval Women

A **lady,** or noblewoman, was told what to do by her father or husband. Ladies did little work. Women in villages worked on the land or as servants. Women in towns worked in almost all jobs.

© Scott Foresman 6

Lesson 3: Review

1. **Main Idea and Details** Fill in the missing main idea that is supported by the details.

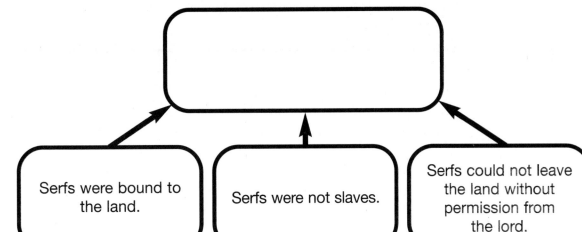

2. Name the four levels in feudalism.

_____

_____

_____

3. What was the purpose of a craft guild?

_____

_____

_____

4. Identify some ways in which feudalism and the manor system affected the lives of the nobility.

_____

_____

_____

5. **Critical Thinking:** *Make Inferences* What feature of the manor system allowed the growth of towns and cities? Explain.

_____

_____

_____

© Scott Foresman 6

Lesson 4: Crusades, Trade, and The Plague

Vocabulary

epidemic a disease that spreads quickly

The Crusades

During the Middle Ages, Christians and Muslims fought wars against each other. In the mid-1000s, Muslim Seljuk Turks took over many lands in the Byzantine Empire, including Palestine. Christians considered Palestine their Holy Land. They believed that Jesus had lived and preached there. In 1095 the Byzantine emperor asked Pope Urban II for help. The pope asked Christian knights to fight the Turks. Between 1095 and 1214, Christian kings, knights, nobles, and other Christians set up eight military expeditions. These expeditions were called the Crusades. The crusaders fought to win back control of Palestine.

East and West

Some crusaders wanted power, land, and riches for themselves. Some set up states on the eastern shore of the Mediterranean Sea. The Crusades led to more contact between the East and the West. This contact led to more trade.

Trade Grows

In the early Middle Ages people produced most of their own food, clothing, and shelter. Later people began to want and need things they could not get on the manor. Craftspeople and merchants began selling their goods at fairs. Later people set up trade routes for these fairs. In time merchants could get goods from nearby places as well as foreign lands. European trade routes linked to Muslim trade routes. On these routes people could get goods from Africa and Asia Minor. European trade routes also linked to the Silk Road, a trade route through Asia.

The Silk Road

The Silk Road was a group of several different routes that passed through Asia and Arabia. The routes began at the Chinese capital. Traders carried gold, ivory, and precious stones to China. From China came silk, furs, ceramics, jade, bronze objects, lacquer, and iron. Ideas also traveled on the Silk Road. The Chinese learned about Buddhism from people traveling on the Silk Road. People began to use the Silk Road to communicate with other parts of the Mongol Empire.

The Plague

The Plague came to Europe in the fourteenth century. The Plague was a bubonic plague. It was a deadly **epidemic,** or disease that spreads quickly over a wide area. The disease was carried mostly by rats. Fleas bit the rats. The disease was passed on when the fleas bit humans. The flea would live, but the rat and person would die. Some historians believe that the Plague started in Central Asia and spread to China. It spread west along the Silk Road. From 1347 to 1352, the Plague killed about one-fourth to one-third of Europe's population. Serfs became more valuable to lords because there were fewer people. Serfs were treated better.

Lesson 4: Review

1. Cause and Effect Fill in the missing causes and effect in the blanks below.

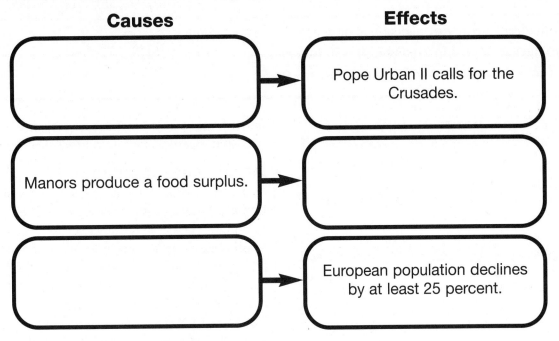

Causes   **Effects**

| | → | Pope Urban II calls for the Crusades. |

| Manors produce a food surplus. | → | |

| | → | European population declines by at least 25 percent. |

2. Who issued the call for the Crusades, and why?

_____

_____

3. In addition to goods, what else traveled along trade routes such as the Silk Road?

_____

_____

4. What caused the Plague? Use the word **epidemic** in your answer.

_____

_____

5. Critical Thinking: *Detect Bias* Why might some historians say that the Plague began in Central Asia?

_____

_____

Lesson 1: The Renaissance

Vocabulary

commerce the buying and selling of a large amount of goods
indulgence a pardon from punishment for sins
excommunicate to expel, or throw out

The Awakening

In 1350 Italy was made up of many separate city-states. The three main city-states were Florence, Milan, and Venice. They were important places for trade and **commerce.** The Renaissance began in Florence in the 1400s. During the Renaissance people had a renewed interest in the art, society, and scientific and political ideas of ancient Greece and Rome. Petrarch was a poet and scholar during the early Renaissance. He encouraged people to study philosophy and literature from the past. He wanted people to speak and write thoughtfully. The Renaissance spread to other European countries by the 1600s.

Art in the Renaissance

The work of Renaissance painters and sculptors was more realistic than the art of medieval Europe. For example, people in paintings now looked more like how people really look. Some famous artists of the Renaissance were Raphael, Michelangelo, and Leonardo da Vinci.

Revolution in Science

Renaissance thinkers believed that people should use reason and the scientific method to understand how the world works. Copernicus and Galileo were important Renaissance scientists. They were astronomers. They both believed that Earth moved around the sun. Copernicus was the first to write about this. Galileo spoke out in favor of Copernicus's ideas. The Catholic Church criticized Galileo. The telescope was invented in 1609. In 1610 Galileo became the first person to use the telescope to study the sky. Galileo's studies challenged the authority of the Catholic Church. Galileo was put on trial and lived under house arrest for the rest of his life. Yet he was able to make many important discoveries.

Renaissance Inventions

In the mid-1400s, Johannes Gutenberg made an important advance in technology. He invented a printing press that used movable type. It used small reusable metal pieces to print each letter and number. Before this, books were copied by hand. The press could make books faster and more cheaply. More people learned how to read. The book trade grew and the economy got stronger. Other inventions of this period include the watch, the single lens microscope, and the thermometer.

The Need for Church Reform

The Roman Catholic Church was wealthy. With that wealth came corruption. Scholars were angry that the church gave **indulgences** for money. This meant that the church would forgive sins if people paid the church. Martin Luther spoke out against the church. Luther believed that Christians should not be judged by their deeds. They should be judged by their belief in God. In 1517 he wrote a challenge to the church. He attacked the sale of indulgences. Luther also wrote that people should be free to interpret the Bible on their own. The church felt that only church leaders could interpret the Bible. The church **excommunicated,** or threw out, Luther. Many people agreed with Luther. His followers became known as Lutherans. Soon other groups of people left the Roman Catholic Church. These events were called the Reformation because these people wanted to reform, or change, the church. They were called Protestants. Christians then became Catholics or Protestants.

© Scott Foresman 6

Lesson 1: Review

1. **Summarize** Write three short sentences that lead to the summary.

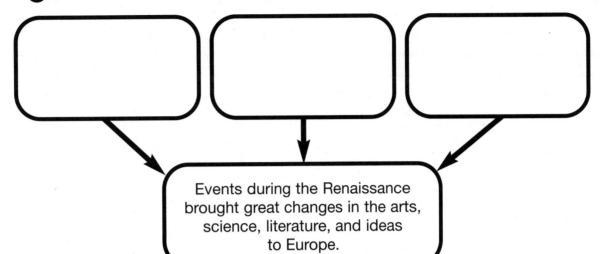

Events during the Renaissance brought great changes in the arts, science, literature, and ideas to Europe.

2. How did Petrarch influence the Renaissance?

_____

_____

_____

3. What practices of the Roman Catholic Church led to the Reformation?

_____

_____

_____

4. How does the Renaissance affect us today?

_____

_____

_____

5. **Critical Thinking:** *Make Inferences* How did the Renaissance change people's thinking? Use the word **commerce** in your answer.

_____

_____

_____

© Scott Foresman 6

Lesson 2: Trade Routes and Conquests

Vocabulary

circumnavigate to sail completely around
conquistador a Spanish conqueror

Portuguese Explorers

In the 1400s Europeans looked upon Africa as a source of gold and other riches. Portugal did not want its traders to travel to Africa on land routes controlled by Muslims. It began to look for sea routes. Prince Henry of Portugal sent many expeditions to western Africa. He hoped to build colonies there. He wanted to end Muslim control of trade. Bartolomeu Dias was a Portuguese explorer. In 1488 he sailed around the Cape of Good Hope, which is at the southern tip of Africa. In 1497 Vasco da Gama sailed around the Cape of Good Hope to India. Da Gama's trip was the first all-water trade route between Europe and Asia. Portugal became an important trading power in the Indian Ocean. Ferdinand Magellan was another Portuguese explorer. In 1519 he set out to sail around the world. He was killed before he could finish the voyage. One of Magellan's ships was able to **circumnavigate,** or sail completely around, the world.

East to West

Christopher Columbus was an Italian explorer. Queen Isabella of Spain gave him money to find a western route to Asia. She wanted to spread Christianity. She also wanted to compete with Portugal for wealth. Columbus left Spain on August 3, 1492. He saw land on October 12. He thought he had reached Asia. He actually saw an island in today's West Indies.

Conquering the Americas

In 1452 the church allowed explorers to enslave the people living in newly-explored lands. Missionaries started going on expeditions. These missionaries tried to bring Christianity to native peoples. The church also helped to write the Treaty of Tordesillas. This treaty divided the Americas between Spain and Portugal. Spanish and Portuguese explorers thought there were riches in the Americas. Hernando Cortes and Francisco Pizarro were **conquistadors.** They became rich after taking over wealthy lands. Conquerors also learned of the food grown by Native Americans, such as maize (corn), tomatoes, potatoes, chocolate, and squash. The Europeans also showed Native Americans their foods, such as wheat, sugar cane, cattle, pigs, and horses. The exchange of plants, animals, and other goods between Europe and the Americas was called the Columbian Exchange. The Columbian Exchange also involved the exchange of disease. Europeans brought new diseases that killed many Native Americans.

The Spanish Armada

Queen Elizabeth of England made England a sea power. She paid for many voyages. Some English explorers also were pirates. They attacked Spanish ships carrying riches. Elizabeth supported the Dutch Protestants who were fighting against Spanish Catholics. All of these things angered King Philip II of Spain. In 1588 he sent the Armada to attack England. The Armada was a large group of warships. The English ships were faster and had powerful guns. They beat the Armada in a few days.

Lesson 2: Review

1. **Summarize** Fill in the summary from the details given below.

```
┌─────────────────┐   ┌─────────────────┐   ┌─────────────────┐
│  The Portuguese │   │ Columbus sailed │   │ Magellan's crew │
│ explored sea    │   │ west to reach   │   │ sailed around   │
│ routes to India.│   │ Asia.           │   │ the world.      │
└─────────────────┘   └─────────────────┘   └─────────────────┘
           ↘                  ↓                  ↙
              ┌──────────────────────────┐
              │                          │
              │                          │
              │                          │
              └──────────────────────────┘
```

2. Why were Europeans interested in exploring Africa?

_____

_____

3. Where is the Cape of Good Hope?

_____

_____

4. What was the Columbian Exchange?

_____

_____

5. **Critical Thinking:** *Make Inferences* What do you think would have happened if the first Spanish explorers had been convinced there was little or no gold to be found in the Americas? Use the word **conquistador** in your answer.

_____

_____

Lesson 3: European Colonization

Vocabulary

colony a settlement that is physically separate from, but under the control of, a ruling country

mercantilism an economic policy in which a country uses colonies to become wealthy and powerful

Early Colonization

Europeans wanted faster routes to the east. While exploring, they made contact with new peoples. Europeans often wanted to use the resources in the lands they explored. These resources included gold, silver, and ivory. Resources also included crops to sell and people to grow the crops. European explorers wanted other Europeans to settle in their conquered lands. They wanted them to run farms and watch over the work. These settlements were **colonies.** The Europeans used **mercantilism** in the colonies. In this system, a country used colonies to get raw materials. The colonies also provided new markets. The colonies could trade only with the country that ruled them. This system made the ruling country very rich.

Portugal and Spain

In the 1500s Portugal and Spain wanted to set up colonies in the Americas. Brazil was the first Portuguese colony. Many Portuguese moved to Brazil so they could own land. Spain formed a new colony in the area where they defeated the Aztecs. They spread Christianity. They also made the Native Americans work. They set up the encomienda. This system gave Spanish colonists the right to make Native Americans in a certain area work for them.

English Colonies

England also wanted colonies. Some English people wanted to gain wealth. Others were looking to set up colonies so they could have religious and political freedom. In 1607 the first successful English colony was set up at Jamestown. By 1732 England had 13 colonies in North America. By that time England was part of Great Britain. The British also established New South Wales in Australia. Great Britain wanted to relieve crowding in British prisons. It sent prisoners to this colony.

French Colonies

France explored Canada in the 1530s. In 1608 the French set up their first permanent settlement in North America. It was called Quebec. The French, British, and Native Americans fought to control land. In 1763 a war broke out among these groups. Great Britain won. It gained all of Canada.

The Slave Trade

Portugal and Spain made slaves of many of the Native Americans living in their colonies. But these countries wanted more workers. Europeans began bringing slaves from Africa to the Americas. Africans were first brought to Virginia in 1619. At first, many Africans were servants. They would be freed after working for a period of years. By the 1640s most Africans who were brought to the colonies were slaves. In the late 1600s, colonial traders sold goods to West African leaders for slaves. Colonial ships brought slaves from Africa to the West Indies. The slaves were then sold for sugar cane. The sugar cane was sent to New England. This type of trade was called the triangular trade. The trip from Africa to the Americas was called the Middle Passage. Many enslaved Africans died on this long, horrible voyage. Most slaves were sent to work on plantations. They worked very hard under bad conditions.

© Scott Foresman 6

Lesson 3: Review

1. ⟳ **Summarize** Fill in the missing details that lead to the summary.

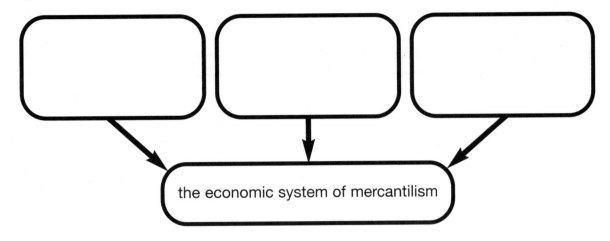

the economic system of mercantilism

2. What are colonies and how did they make European countries wealthy and powerful?

_____

_____

_____

3. What was the encomienda?

_____

_____

_____

4. What were some of the reasons for European colonization?

_____

_____

_____

5. **Critical Thinking:** *Solve Complex Problems* How could Europeans have colonized other lands without forcing the native peoples to work for them?

_____

_____

_____

Lesson 1: Revolutions in the Americas

Vocabulary

legislature a lawmaking body
massacre an event that causes the death of unresisting or helpless people

The Roots of Conflict

For a long time, the 13 British colonies in North America largely governed themselves. Each colony had a **legislature** that made laws. Great Britain began taxing the colonies. The colonists were angry that Great Britain forced them to pay taxes without their consent. Many colonists shouted, "No taxation without representation!" In 1770 colonists in Boston yelled at British soldiers and threw stones at them. Some of the soldiers fired their guns and killed several colonists. This event was called the Boston Massacre. A **massacre** is an event that causes the death of unresisting or helpless people. New laws also angered colonists. Under one of these laws, colonists could buy tea from only one company. In 1773 some Boston colonists protested this law. They threw tea into Boston Harbor. This was known as the Boston Tea Party. Great Britain then closed the port and sent more troops to Boston.

The American Revolution

The colonists wanted to govern themselves. They decided to declare their independence. Leaders wrote the Declaration of Independence. The Declaration stated why the colonies wanted independence. It was approved on July 4, 1776. The American Revolution had begun. In the American Revolution, the Americans fought the British for their freedom. The Americans won many important battles. George Washington was an American general. He forced British troops to surrender at Yorktown. In 1783 the British agreed that the United States was an independent nation.

Revolution in Haiti

Haiti was a French colony on an island in Latin America. In 1791 African slaves in Haiti revolted against French rule. Toussaint L'Ouverture led the revolt. The slaves forced the French to leave Haiti. In 1802 the French tried to recapture Haiti. They failed, and the Haitians declared independence in 1804. Haiti became the first independent country in Latin America.

The Revolution Spreads

Father Miguel Hidalgo was a priest in Mexico. In 1810 he asked people in Dolores, Mexico, to revolt against Spanish rule. Many Mexicans began fighting for independence from Spain. Hidalgo's words spread through Latin America. Latin Americans wanted political and economic freedom. They were not allowed to rule themselves. Latin Americans could trade only with Spain. They could move goods only on Spanish ships.

Independence for Mexico and Central America

Father Hidalgo was killed in 1811, but the fighting continued. In 1821 Mexico gained independence from Spain. Then Central America defeated Spain. Central Americans formed the United Provinces of Central America in 1823. This group later split into separate nations.

Independence for South America

The fight for South American independence took many years. Simón Bolívar was a South American leader. For 15 years Bolívar led his army through hot rain forests and over rugged mountains. Bolívar helped free Peru and many other South American countries. José de San Martín and Bernardo O'Higgins were other important leaders. They worked together to free Chile from Spanish rule. By the 1820s almost all of Latin America was independent.

Lesson 1: Review

1. **Compare and Contrast** Fill in the diagram below to compare and contrast the revolutions in the Americas.

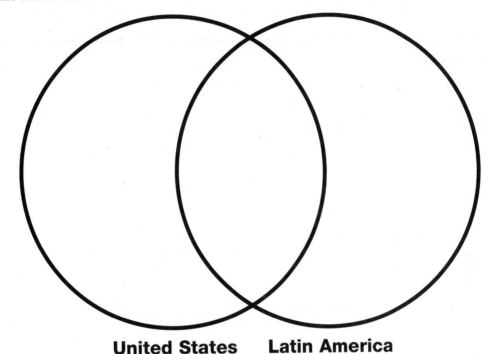

United States   Latin America

2. Why did the American colonists believe that they needed to break free of British rule?

   _____

   _____

3. Who was Father Miguel Hidalgo?

   _____

   _____

4. Name two restrictions that the Spanish government put on the people of Latin America.

   _____

   _____

5. **Critical Thinking:** *Evaluate Information* Why do you think the fight for South American independence took so many years?

   _____

   _____

© Scott Foresman 6

Lesson 2: The French Revolution

Vocabulary

monarchy a government in which a king, queen, or emperor has supreme power

France in Trouble

In the mid-1700s, France's **monarchy** was falling apart. A monarchy is a government in which a king, queen, or emperor has supreme power. France's tax system was unfair. Peasants and the middle class paid high taxes. Nobles paid almost none. King Louis XVI called a meeting of the Estates-General. The Estates-General was a group of the king's advisors. It was made up of France's three estates, or classes. The First Estate was made up of church leaders. The Second Estate was made up of nobles. The Third Estate was made up of the rest of the people in France. About 98 percent of the people belonged to the Third Estate. Yet each estate had one vote. The First and Second Estate could outvote the Third Estate. This meant that a few church leaders and nobles had more power than almost all of the people in France put together. The Third Estate wanted every person at the meeting to have a vote. The king would not allow this. The people in the Third Estate were angry. They formed the National Assembly. This started the French Revolution.

New and Old Privileges

King Louis began gathering troops near the National Assembly's meeting. This angered people in Paris, France. They attacked a prison called the Bastille and stole its weapons. The National Assembly made nobles and church leaders pay taxes. It also said that peasants would no longer have to work for the nobles without pay. In 1789 the National Assembly wrote a *Declaration of the Rights of Man and of Citizen.* It was inspired by the U.S. Declaration of Independence. It gave all men equal rights, such as freedom of speech and religion. Other European rulers were worried the revolution would spread. They sent troops to France and

fought the French army. Many people in France began to panic.

The Reign of Terror

In 1792 new leaders took control away from the king. They made France a republic. They killed King Louis and the queen, Marie Antoinette. This began the Reign of Terror. It was a time of violence. People thought to be against the revolution were put to death. Maximilien de Robespierre led the committee that took over the government. The committee executed people it suspected of opposing the revolution. The committee killed about 40,000 people in one year. Robespierre himself was killed near the end of the Reign of Terror. Yet the republic made some advances. Slavery was ended in all French colonies. The wealthy also had special privileges taken away.

Napoleon

In 1799 Napoleon Bonaparte overthrew the republic. By 1804 he was emperor of France. He made the government strong. He brought back order. He made a new set of laws for France. It was called the Napoleonic Code. The Code is still the basis of French law today. It was based on Roman laws and some reforms made during the republic.

Napoleon's Conquests

Napoleon wanted to build his own empire. Napoleon's army took over many parts of Europe. In 1812 the French Empire began to weaken. Many French soldiers died when they tried to invade Russia. Other countries joined together to defeat Napoleon. They forced him out of France.

Lesson 2: Review

1. ⟳ **Summarize** Write a brief summary of the main points that led to the French Revolution.

| The French monarchy had too much power. | The Estates-General did not give equal representation to the estates. | France's tax system was unfair. |

2. How did Napoleon improve conditions in France?

_____

_____

_____

3. Who was Robespierre?

_____

_____

_____

4. What accomplishments did the republic bring to France?

_____

_____

_____

5. **Critical Thinking:** *Recognize Point of View* Why would other European leaders band together to defeat Napoleon?

_____

_____

_____

Lesson 3: The Industrial Revolution

Vocabulary

textile cloth that is either woven or knitted

factory a place where products are made with machines

tenement overcrowded slum apartments

A New Way of Making Things

Before 1750 people or animals did most of the work. Things often were made at home. For example, people brought home cotton to make **textiles,** or cloth that is woven or knitted. After 1750 the people in Europe began using machines to make goods. This change from human or animal power to machine power was called the Industrial Revolution. The Industrial Revolution began with the invention of the steam engine. This occurred in Great Britain in the early 1700s. In the 1760s James Watt improved the steam engine. Now it could power large machines. Later machines were grouped together in one place, a **factory.**

Great Britain and the Steam Engine

There were many reasons why the Industrial Revolution began in Great Britain. Great Britain had important natural resources such as coal and iron. It had many skilled workers. Many people in Great Britain had money to invest in factories. Great Britain had a good transportation network. This is a system of roads and rivers to move goods. Great Britain also had colonies. These colonies supplied Great Britain with raw materials and bought its goods. In 1825 George Stephenson invented a train run by a steam engine. This began the "Railroad Age." Robert Fulton built the first successful steamboat. By the 1840s steamships were crossing the Atlantic Ocean.

Terrible Conditions

Early factories were dark and dirty. People worked very long hours. Most workers were women and children. They were paid much less than men. The factories were dangerous. Machines had few or no safety devices. One of the most dangerous jobs involved crawling under running machines. Many people were hurt. Coal was a source of cheap fuel. It helped power the Industrial Revolution. Coal mines were dangerous places to work.

Growing Cities Have Many Problems

Between 1800 and 1850, Europe's population grew quickly. After the Industrial Revolution began, many people moved from farms or villages to cities such as London, England. At this time farms used more machines. Fewer farm workers were needed. These workers found jobs in the growing number of city factories. Many of these workers lived in **tenements,** or overcrowded slum apartments. The tenements did not offer many public services, such as garbage collection. Many slums were dirty and unhealthy places to live.

Lesson 3: Review

1. **Compare and Contrast** Fill in the diagram to compare and contrast the way goods were made before and after the Industrial Revolution.

Before   **After**

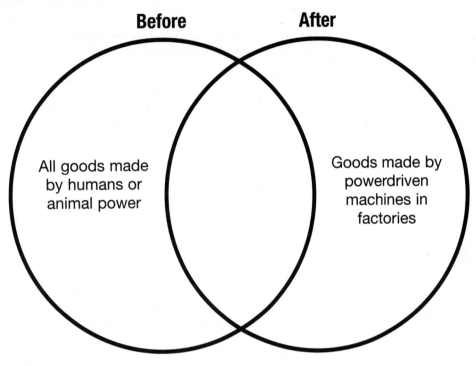

All goods made by humans or animal power

Goods made by powerdriven machines in factories

2. What did James Watt's improvements to the steam engine accomplish?

_____

_____

3. What factors allowed Great Britain to get a head start in the Industrial Revolution?

_____

_____

4. Why did so many people move to cities between 1800 and 1850?

_____

_____

5. **Critical Thinking:** *Make Inferences* Why do you think the conditions were so bad in London factories and London slums?

_____

_____

© Scott Foresman 6

Lesson 4: The Second Industrial Revolution

Vocabulary

corporation a business organization that raises money by selling parts of the company to the public

reformer a person who wanted to improve, or reform, capitalism

strike the refusal to work until demands are met

New Sources of Power

The Second Industrial Revolution began after the 1850s. It was powered by oil, electricity, and steel. Thomas Edison helped create many inventions we use today. These include the light bulb, phonograph (the ancestor of the CD player), and movie camera. Bridges and buildings were made stronger with steel. Oil was used for lighting, heating, and to power automobile engines. Electricity was used for light and to power machines. Electricity led to the invention of the telephone and radio.

Corporations and Assembly Lines

By the early 1800s, it cost a lot of money to open a factory. People needed a way to raise this money. They developed a new type of business organization. It was called a **corporation.** Corporations raised millions of dollars by selling parts of the company to the public. These parts were called stock shares. If the corporation made money, then part of this money was given to the shareholders. In the early 1900s, Henry Ford developed the assembly line. On the assembly line, a product moved past a number of workers. Each worker added a part to the product. In this way products could be made more quickly.

Capitalism and Reformers

An economic system called capitalism developed during the Industrial Revolution. Under capitalism people, not the government, own most factories and industries. The type of capitalism that grew at this time was a market economy. In a market economy, people decide

how to spend their own money. Business owners build their businesses around what people want to buy. Most capitalists wanted to run their businesses freely. They did not want any government controls. People called **reformers** were upset about poor conditions in factories. They thought capitalism could be improved with government help.

Working Conditions

Reformers got governments in Europe and North America to make changes. They passed laws that improved working and living conditions. Many workers formed labor unions to improve conditions. Labor unions speak for all the workers in a factory. Unions used **strikes** to get what they wanted. A strike is a refusal to work. In Great Britain laws were passed to ban labor unions. But by the late 1800s, the unions were strong.

The Socialists

Some people wanted to replace capitalism with an economic system called socialism. Under socialism the government owns most industries, businesses, land, and natural resources. Most socialists wanted to make changes in a peaceful way. But some wanted to revolt against the government. One of these people was Karl Marx. Marx was a German socialist. He made socialist ideas popular. Marx believed there would be a worldwide revolution. After this revolution there would be no separate economic classes. Working conditions improved in the 1800s and 1900s. Many workers did not see any reason to revolt.

© Scott Foresman 6

Name _____ Date _____

Lesson 4: Review

1. **Main Idea and Details** Fill in the diagram to give examples of familiar machines that were invented during the Second Industrial Revolution.

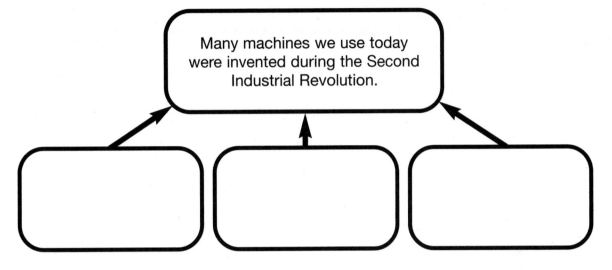

Many machines we use today were invented during the Second Industrial Revolution.

2. What is a corporation?

_____

_____

3. Why did reformers want to improve working conditions?

_____

_____

4. Who was Karl Marx?

_____

_____

5. **Critical Thinking:** *Make Generalizations* Do you believe that Thomas Edison's inventions improved people's lives? Explain your answer.

_____

_____

Lesson 1: Expanding Empires

Vocabulary

nationalism a strong devotion to one's own country
imperialism when one country builds an empire by controlling or taking over other lands
imperialist a person who supports imperialism

Nationalism and Imperialism

In the 1800s the idea of **nationalism** spread through Europe. Nationalism is a strong devotion to a person's own country. For some people, nationalism meant wanting their country to be stronger. For others it meant feeling that their country was better than others. Nationalism often was connected to the idea of imperialism. **Imperialism** meant one country building an empire by taking over other lands. Imperialism also took hold in Europe in the 1800s. During this time European countries took over lands in Africa, Asia, and elsewhere. European countries made these lands their colonies. The Europeans made money from these colonies. They took raw materials such as cotton and oil from the colonies. They also sold European goods to the colonies. European **imperialists** believed imperialism was a good thing. They thought it was good to bring Christianity and European ways to other areas of the world. Imperialists thought their ways would help non-European people become more advanced. Cecil Rhodes was a British imperialist in South Africa. He thought that Europeans were better than non-Europeans. He wanted to teach European ways to as much of the world as possible.

Empires in Asia and Africa

Great Britain had the world's largest empire in the 1800s. It had colonies all over the world. India was Great Britain's most valuable colony. India held many riches. Britain had ruled part of India since the 1600s. Many Indians did not like British rule. They revolted in 1857. This revolt was called the Indian Mutiny. The British stopped the revolt. Great Britain then spread its empire to Egypt. The British took control of a new waterway there, the Suez Canal. The canal was built by the French. It shortened the distance from Great Britain to India. France and the Netherlands took over parts of South and Southeast Asia. In 1884 Great Britain, France, Belgium, Germany, and Italy met at the Berlin Conference. They divided up Africa among themselves. No African countries were invited to the Berlin Conference. After the conference, there were only two African countries that were still independent. Imperialism was very harsh in Africa. For example, Belgium's King Leopold II controlled the Congo region in Africa. He treated the Africans in the Congo Free State very cruelly. After 20 years of Belgian rule, the population in the Congo dropped by about one-half.

© Scott Foresman 6

Lesson 1: Review

1. **Summarize** Fill in the details of the summary.

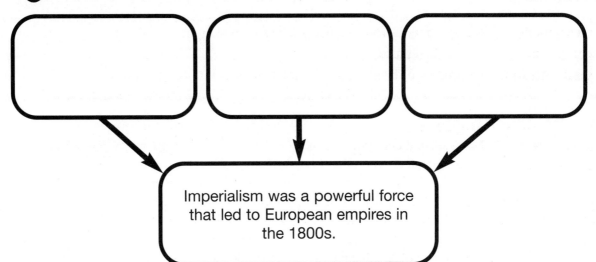

Imperialism was a powerful force that led to European empires in the 1800s.

2. Why did some Europeans believe that imperialism would benefit people in colonies?

_____

_____

_____

3. What evidence could you offer to show that King Leopold's rule in the Congo was harsh?

_____

_____

_____

4. In what parts of the world did Europeans build their empires in the 1800s?

_____

_____

_____

5. **Critical Thinking:** *Detect Bias* Do you think that Cecil Rhodes could back up his opinion with solid evidence? Why or why not?

_____

_____

_____

Lesson 2: Imperialism in East Asia

Vocabulary

treaty port a port city where Europeans had special trading rights
compound an area that is set aside
modernization the process of bringing ways and standards into the present day

The Middle Kingdom

China viewed itself as a special country. It kept its customs and culture separated from other cultures. China wanted very little contact with Europe. Therefore, its trade with Europe was strictly controlled. The Chinese traditionally believed that their country was surrounded by people who were inferior, or not as advanced. That is why the Chinese word for China means "Middle Kingdom." The Qing dynasty began to rule China in 1644. This dynasty worked to keep European ideas out of China. By the 1800s China's technology had fallen far behind that of European countries. Chinese boats and weapons were not as good. Because of this the Chinese were unable to keep foreigners and imperialism out of China.

Western Imperialists in China

The British began bringing opium into China in the late 1700s. China wanted Great Britain to stop bringing opium to the country, but Great Britain would not stop. This began the first Opium War. The British won the war in 1842. China gave Hong Kong to Great Britain. The British made China open five **treaty ports** where Europeans had special trade rights. The Europeans ran their own **compounds** in these ports. The second Opium War was fought in the late 1850s. France joined Great Britain and defeated China again. As a result more treaty ports were opened for European trading. Other European countries also began taking over parts of China. The Chinese people did not like European imperialism. In 1850 many Chinese revolted. This revolt was stopped, but millions of Chinese died. In 1894 China went to war with Japan. China was defeated. In 1898

another revolt broke out. It involved "the Boxers," a powerful group of Chinese rebels who wanted to get rid of all foreign influences in China. The Europeans sent an army into China's capital, Beijing. They stopped the revolt. The United States also was interested in China. It set up an Open Door Policy. This policy gave every country the same chance to trade with China. The policy helped foreigners control China.

Japan and the West

In 1853 U.S. naval officer Matthew Perry brought warships to Japan. He also brought a letter. In the letter the U.S. President demanded that Japan open treaty ports. Japan opened the ports in 1854. Japan had kept itself closed off from the outside world for about 200 years. Emperor Meiji took power in 1868. He started a program of **modernization.** He began to improve Japan's technology to catch up with the West. The Japanese studied Western ways in science and industry. Japan grew stronger. Other countries began to treat Japan better. They ended the unfair port policies. After its war with China in 1895, Japan gained control of the island of Formosa. It later took over Korea.

New World Power

In 1904 Japan went to war with Russia. They fought for control of the northeastern region of China, known as Manchuria. Japan surprised the world by beating Russia. After this the West saw Japan as a world power. A world power is a very strong nation.

© Scott Foresman 6

Lesson 2: Review

1. Cause and Effect Fill in the missing cause and effects.

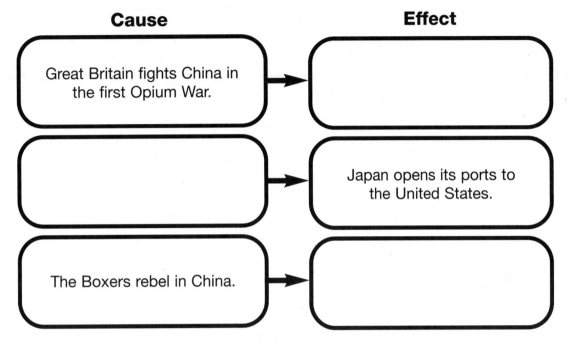

Cause

Effect

Great Britain fights China in the first Opium War.

Japan opens its ports to the United States.

The Boxers rebel in China.

2. What traditional Chinese belief explains the name "Middle Kingdom" for China?

_____

_____

3. How did Japan change after Meiji came to power in 1868?

_____

_____

4. Before the 1800s what contact did China and Japan have with Western countries?

_____

_____

5. Critical Thinking: *Make Inferences* Do you think the Qing dynasty provided the leadership needed to modernize China in the 1800s? Explain your answer.

_____

_____

Lesson 3: New Nations

Vocabulary

> **dominion** a nation that governs itself, but is still connected to a ruling empire
>
> **parliament** a group of elected lawmakers and leaders

Nationalism and Unification

Nationalism encouraged some countries to form new nations. For hundreds of years, Germany and Italy were ruled by different countries and people. The Germans wanted to have their own country. So did the Italians. Many Germans and Italians believed that people who share customs, culture, and a language make up a nation. Italians and Germans were willing to fight to form their own countries. They looked to Greece as an example. For almost 500 years, the Greeks had been ruled by the Ottoman Empire. But the Greeks had a different language, history, and customs. In the 1820s the people of Greece fought a war of independence against the Ottomans. Greece became an independent country in 1830.

A German Nation

Before Germany was unified, or united, it had many states. Prussia was the largest and most powerful of these states. Otto von Bismarck was the prime minister of Prussia. He led three wars to unify Germany. In 1871 Prussia declared Germany a united empire. Prussia's king became the kaiser, or emperor, of unified Germany. Prussia controlled Germany's government. The government was not democratic. Prussia also supported Germany's military and wars. Germany quickly grew into a powerful country. Wilhelm II was a German kaiser. He said that he would continue to fight to keep Germany a world power. Other European nations began to fear Germany's strength.

A United Italy

Nationalism was rising in Italy too. Italians wanted to unify Italy. Giuseppe Mazzini was an Italian leader. He wanted Italians to drive out their rulers and form one democratic government. Another leader was Camillo di Cavour. He was prime minister of the Kingdom of Sardinia. Cavour wanted Italy to unite under Sardinia's King Emmanuel II. In 1859 Cavour joined with France. They drove Austria out of northern Italy. After this, northern Italy agreed to join Sardinia and be ruled by King Emmanuel II. Giuseppe Garibaldi led a small army called the "Redshirts." In 1860 the Redshirts freed southern Italy. Southern Italy united with the rest of Italy. Austria went to war with Prussia in 1866. This helped Italy take control of Venice and Rome. Italy became a unified country in 1870.

British Dominions

In the 1800s many of Great Britain's colonies wanted to rule themselves. Great Britain decided to make some of these colonies **dominions.** A dominion is a nation that governs itself but is still connected to a ruling empire. The government of the dominions was like that of Great Britain. The dominions set up a **parliament,** or a group of elected lawmakers and leaders. Each dominion also had a leader who spoke for the British king or queen. In 1867 Great Britain made Canada its first dominion. The British had set up many colonies in Australia beginning in 1788. Australia was named a dominion in 1901. Australia was later united into a single nation. New Zealand became a British dominion in 1907. New Zealand was first settled by the Maori, a group of Polynesian people. The British and the Maori had fought over land for many years.

© Scott Foresman 6

Lesson 3: Review

1. **Sequence** Put the events in their correct time order.

   _____ Australia became a dominion.

   _____ Canada became a dominion.

   _____ Garibaldi freed southern Italy.

   _____ Germany became an empire.

   _____ Greece became independent.

2. How did the example of Greece give hope to nationalistic Germans and Italians?

   _____

   _____

   _____

   _____

3. What did the German Empire inherit from the powerful German state of Prussia?

   _____

   _____

   _____

   _____

4. How did nationalism lead to the formation of a unified Germany and Italy?

   _____

   _____

   _____

5. **Critical Thinking:** *Evaluate Information* Do you think that the British dominions were truly independent? Explain your answer.

   _____

   _____

   _____

   _____

Lesson 1: Headed Toward War

Vocabulary

mobilization what nations do to prepare for war
neutral not taking sides

Competition Among Nations

Nationalism and imperialism were strong in Europe in the 1800s. This caused European countries to compete with one another. European countries wanted natural resources from colonies. The countries used the resources to help their industries grow. They raced to take over land in Asia, Africa, and other places. But there was little land left to colonize. European nations also rushed to build bigger navies and armies than one another. In the 1890s Germany wanted to build a big navy. This upset the British because they had the biggest navy up to that time. There also were other problems. Germany had taken over two of France's provinces. France wanted the provinces back. Austria-Hungary had many different ethnic groups. These groups wanted countries of their own. In 1908 Austria-Hungary took over two provinces in Serbia. This angered the Serbians.

Alliances Lead to War

European nations joined together to form two alliances. They formed the alliances to protect one another. In 1882 Germany, Austria-Hungary, and Italy formed an alliance called the Triple Alliance. In 1907 Russia, France, and Great Britain formed the Triple Entente. In both alliances an attack on one country was considered an attack on all of the countries. The alliances pushed Europe closer to war. Many countries began to mobilize for war. **Mobilization** is what nations do to prepare for war. In 1914 the Triple Alliance and the Triple Entente had a big disagreement. Then Archduke Francis Ferdinand was assassinated, or murdered, in Bosnia. Francis Ferdinand was an important leader in Austria-Hungary. A man from Serbia had killed him. Therefore, Austria-Hungary wanted to punish Serbia. Russia wanted to protect Serbia. Russia mobilized its army. Germany then declared war on Russia and Russia's ally, France. Germany also invaded Belgium. Belgium was a **neutral** country, or one that does not take sides. Great Britain had an agreement with Belgium. After this invasion Great Britain declared war on Germany. The Great War had begun.

Lesson 1: Review

1. 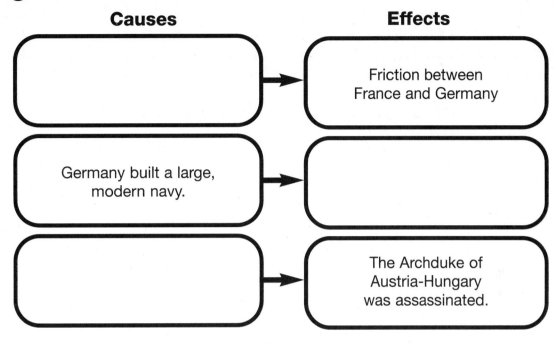 **Cause and Effect** Fill in the chart below by listing one cause or effect.

Causes	Effects
	Friction between France and Germany
Germany built a large, modern navy.	
	The Archduke of Austria-Hungary was assassinated.

2. What strong forces caused friction between the countries of Europe in the years leading up to 1914?

   _____

   _____

3. What was a cause of friction between France and Germany?

   _____

   _____

4. How did imperialism increase competition among nations in Europe?

   _____

   _____

5. **Critical Thinking: *Make Inferences*** Suppose the nations of Europe had not formed alliances in the years before 1914. Do you think a world war would have broken out? Explain. Use the word **neutral** in your answer.

   _____

   _____

© Scott Foresman 6

Lesson 2: The Great War

Vocabulary

casualty a killed or hurt soldier

trench warfare a form of fighting in which armies dig deep trenches, or ditches, to shelter their troops

armistice a stop in fighting

The War Begins

The war lasted about four years, from 1914 to 1918. The Germans fought huge battles against the French and British. But neither side could win or move forward very much. These battles took place on the Western Front. It was located in France. At the same time Russia was fighting against Germany and Austria-Hungary. The line of battle between Russia and Austria-Hungary was called the Eastern Front. In 1914 the Ottoman Empire joined forces with Germany and Austria-Hungary. In 1915 Italy joined Great Britain, France, and Russia. The Triple Alliance was now called the Central Powers. The Triple Entente became the Allied Powers.

A New Kind of War

In the Great War more soldiers were hurt or killed than in any war before it. New weapons caused these **casualties.** These weapons included the machine gun, the airplane, the tank, and poison gas. **Trench warfare** was another reason why the war was so deadly. Whenever soldiers crawled out of their trenches, enemy soldiers fired on them. Two of the worst battles took place in 1916. Germany attacked Verdun, France. About 500,000 soldiers died. Germany gained very little from the battle. The second big battle was Great Britain's attack on German forces at the Somme River. The British lost about 20,000 soldiers in one day. The Allies gained very little from this battle as well.

Women's War Work

Women played an important role in the war. In Great Britain women taught soldiers how to use gas masks. They also drove ambulances, were nurses, worked in factories, and grew crops. In Germany women sewed uniforms and bed sheets for the soldiers. They also worked as nurses.

America Enters

Two events brought the United States into the war. Germany sank British and American ships. Then, the United States learned that Germany asked Mexico to join the Central Powers. In return Germany would give land to Mexico. The United States then declared war on Germany. In 1918 the United States sent troops to France. The Allies began to win. In November 1918 Germany agreed to an **armistice.** The fighting was over.

The Russian Revolution

The Russian army had many casualties on the Eastern Front. Things were also very bad inside Russia. The Russian people had little fuel and food. In 1917 the Russian Revolution broke out. Czar Nicholas II was forced out of power. Vladimir Lenin led a group known as the Bolsheviks, or communists. He promised the Russian people peace, bread, and land. The communists took power. They followed communism, a system in which the state controls all property. Lenin signed a treaty with Germany. In 1922 the communists formed the Soviet Union.

Another Victory

After the Great War soldiers returned home. Most women stopped working. But women in many countries now had the right to vote in national elections. This included women in the United States.

© Scott Foresman 6

Lesson 2: Review

1. **Cause and Effect** Fill in the chart below by listing two causes that convinced the United States to enter the Great War.

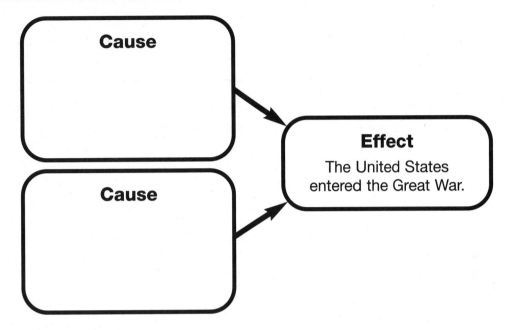

2. What new weapons made the Great War deadlier than earlier wars?

_____

_____

3. What did Lenin and the communists promise the Russian people to gain their support in the Russian Revolution?

_____

_____

4. How do the battles of Verdun and the Somme summarize the experience of the Great War?

_____

_____

5. **Critical Thinking:** *Make Inferences* Given the terrible casualties in the Great War battles, do you think that some people questioned whether winning was worth the cost? Why or why not?

_____

_____

© Scott Foresman 6

Lesson 3: After the War

Vocabulary

holocaust a mass killing
reparation payment for war losses
inflation the rapid increase in prices

Results of the War

Millions of soldiers and other people died in the Great War. The war destroyed many homes and businesses. Nations owed vast amounts of money because of the war. The war changed the map of Europe. Many empires in Eastern Europe were gone. This included the German Empire, the Russian Empire, and the Ottoman Empire. In Turkey the government killed a huge number of Armenians, a minority group. This event was called the Armenian **Holocaust**.

Making Peace

In 1919 the United States, Great Britain, France, and Italy met in Paris to discuss peace. President Woodrow Wilson had a plan for peace. It was called the Fourteen Points. Wilson hoped his plan would prevent future wars. President Wilson wanted peace and cooperation between all nations. Georges Clemenceau was the leader of France.

Clemenceau disagreed with President Wilson's plan. He wanted to weaken Germany so that it would never again threaten France. The two leaders finally agreed on another plan. It was called the Treaty of Versailles. In the treaty was Wilson's idea for a group of nations to prevent war. This became the League of Nations. Under the Treaty of Versailles, Germany had to remove its forts and other defenses from the Rhineland. The Rhineland was on the border between France and Germany. The treaty also made Germany accept blame for starting the war. It forced Germany to pay huge **reparations,** or payments. These reparations would help the Allies pay for the war. But Germany did not have the money to make these payments. Because of these payments Germany experienced very high **inflation.** German money became almost worthless. The people suffered.

Use with pages 534–537.

Lesson 3: Review

1. 🔄 **Cause and Effect** Fill in the chart below by listing two effects in the blank boxes.

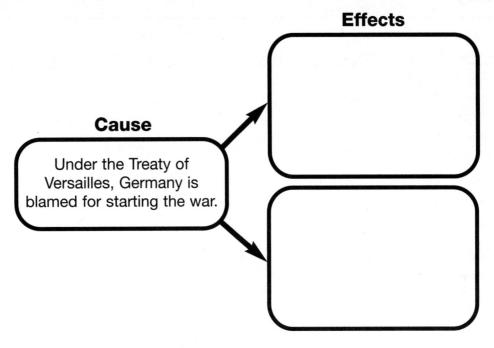

Effects

Cause

Under the Treaty of Versailles, Germany is blamed for starting the war.

2. What part of Europe was most affected by boundary changes after the Great War?

_____

_____

3. In what ways did the Treaty of Versailles punish Germany?

_____

_____

4. What was the major stumbling block in establishing the kind of fair and just peace that President Wilson wanted?

_____

_____

5. Critical Thinking: *Solve Complex Problems* What impact did paying reparations to the Allies have on Germany's economy?

_____

_____

© Scott Foresman 6

Lesson 1: Good to Bad Times

Vocabulary

depression a time when the economy does badly and many people become poor

fascism a form of government in which the nation is more important than individuals

Nazi the fascist party in Germany

propaganda the planned spread of certain ideas; ideas are spread through posters, pamphlets, or speeches

aggression the act of attacking other countries

annex to attach one country to another

appeasement a policy that meets the demands of an attacker in order to keep peace

collective farms that are grouped together and run by the government

The 1920s

During the war American farmers took out loans to buy more land. After the war the farmers did not make enough money to pay back the loans. Other Americans also borrowed money that they could not pay back. They could not buy goods. Factories stopped making goods. People lost their jobs. Prices fell quickly. Many banks and businesses closed. The Great Depression began. During a **depression** there are very few jobs. People are not able to buy the things they need, such as food. The Great Depression affected many countries.

New Dictators in Europe

Italy and Germany were in bad shape after the war. A new political movement formed in these troubled countries. It was called **fascism.** Benito Mussolini led the fascists in Italy. He said he would make things better for Italy. In October 1922 he took over as dictator of Italy. Germany was still paying reparations when the Great Depression hit. Millions of Germans did not have jobs. Many joined Germany's fascist party. This party was called the **Nazis.** Adolf Hitler led the Nazis. In 1933 Hitler became dictator of Germany. Hitler and the Nazis used **propaganda** to control the German people.

Steps Toward War

Mussolini and Hitler followed a policy of **aggression.** This meant they attacked other

countries. In 1935 Italy and Germany helped Spanish fascists beat the Spanish government. Hitler sent troops to the Rhineland. In March 1938 German troops took over Austria. They **annexed,** or attached, it to Germany. All of these acts were not allowed under the Treaty of Versailles. But neither France nor Great Britain did much to stop Germany. In September 1938 Hitler claimed part of Czechoslovakia. Germany agreed to make no more claims in Europe. This agreement grew out of an idea called **appeasement.** It met Germany's demands in order to keep peace. In 1939 Hitler broke the agreement. He took the rest of Czechoslovakia.

Japan Seizes an Empire

In 1930 Japan's leaders wanted their own raw materials. In 1931 Japan took over Manchuria, a region in northeastern China. It was rich in coal and iron. In 1937 Japan began a war against all of China. Japan's leaders planned to take over all of eastern and southeastern Asia.

A Soviet Dictator

The Soviet leader Lenin died in 1924. Joseph Stalin became dictator. Stalin joined farms into **collectives.** The farmers revolted when Stalin began combining their farms. Stalin sent many of them to prison camps or killed them. Farm production fell. Many people starved. Stalin began a program called the Great Terror. Millions of people were killed or sent to work camps.

Lesson 1: Review

1. ⟳ **Cause and Effect** Fill in the chart below by listing one important effect or cause.

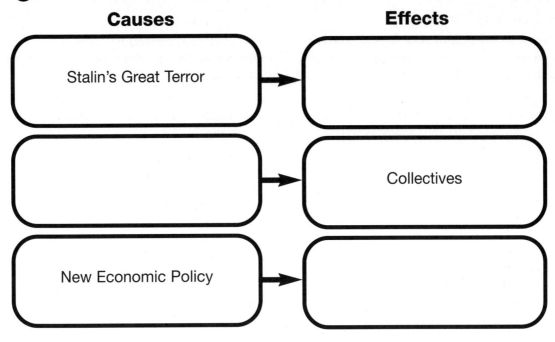

Causes

Effects

Stalin's Great Terror →

→ Collectives

New Economic Policy →

2. Explain how inflation and the Great Depression affected world economies.

_____

_____

3. Define fascism and name two fascist countries from this lesson.

_____

_____

4. How did hard times lead to the rise of dictators in Italy and Germany?

_____

_____

5. **Critical Thinking:** *Make Inferences* Why do you think that Hitler repeatedly violated the Treaty of Versailles?

_____

_____

Lesson 2: World War II

World War II Begins

In September 1939 German troops invaded Poland. Great Britain and France declared war on Germany. World War II had begun. Germany continued to invade European countries. One of these countries was France. France surrendered quickly. Great Britain was left to fight Germany alone. Italy had joined Germany's side too. Then Germany began to use airplanes to attack Great Britain. But Britain's Royal Air Force was too powerful. The Germans gave up on Great Britain. In June 1941 Hitler invaded the Soviet Union. The Germans were not prepared for the cold Soviet winter. They left the Soviet Union by 1943.

The United States Enters the War

In 1940 President Franklin Roosevelt worried that the Axis Powers would win the war. The Axis Powers were Germany, Italy, and Japan. To help the Allies, the United States sold them war supplies. The Allies were Great Britain, the Soviet Union, and China. The United States also stopped exporting goods to Japan. Japan led a surprise attack on the United States on December 7, 1941. The attack happened at Pearl Harbor in Hawaii. The United States then declared war on Japan. Germany and Italy declared war on the United States. Many Americans became angry with all Japanese people. This included Japanese Americans. In 1942 Roosevelt ordered all people of Japanese background to be taken to prison camps.

Women in the War

Many women worked in factories that made weapons. The Women's Air Force Service Pilots was an American group. Its members flew aircraft to military bases all over the world. The Soviet Union allowed women to fight because there were not enough men left. Some British women served in the military, but did not fight. German women worked as nurses or in other jobs that did not involve fighting.

The Tide Turns

Allied leaders agreed to try to beat Germany before Japan. In late 1942 the British stopped the Axis Powers from moving into Egypt. From there the Allies invaded southern Italy. The Germans and the Soviets fought a long battle in the Soviet Union. The Germans surrendered this battle in February 1943. It was another turning point in the war.

Victory in Europe

During the war millions of Americans served in the armed forces. The United States produced a huge number of tanks and airplanes. June 6, 1944, was D-Day. On this day the Allied troops began the largest invasion by sea ever. Thousands of ships came from southern Great Britain to Normandy, France. American and French troops drove the Germans out of France. Soviet forces drove the Germans out of the Soviet Union and nearly all of Eastern Europe. Nazi Germany surrendered to the Allies on May 7, 1945.

Toward Victory Over Japan

After the attack on Pearl Harbor, two sea battles stopped the Japanese from advancing across the Pacific Ocean. The first was the Battle of Coral Sea. The second was the Battle of Midway. It was the first Allied victory in the Pacific.

Dropping the Atomic Bomb

Japan fought back with a new weapon called the kamikaze. Kamikazes were pilots who flew their planes into enemy warships. They sank many Allied ships. On August 6, 1945, the United States dropped an atomic bomb on the city of Hiroshima, Japan. Thousands of Japanese died. Huge numbers of buildings were destroyed. On August 9, the United States dropped another atomic bomb on the city of Nagasaki. Japan surrendered on September 2, 1945. World War II was over.

Lesson 2: Review

1. ⟳ **Cause and Effect** Fill in the chart below with one effect of Hitler's attacks on the countries shown.

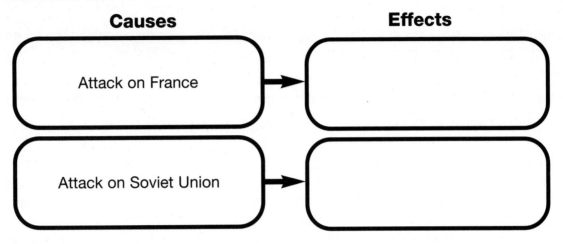

Causes   **Effects**

Attack on France

Attack on Soviet Union

2. What made Hitler give up on invading Great Britain?

_____

_____

_____

3. What was significant about D-Day?

_____

_____

_____

4. What effect did dropping the atomic bomb have on Japan?

_____

_____

_____

5. **Critical Thinking:** *Evaluate Information* What do you think might have happened if the United States had not entered the war in Europe? Explain your answer.

_____

_____

_____

Lesson 3: The Aftermath

Vocabulary

refugee a person who leaves his or her homeland for a safer place

concentration camp a place that held imprisoned people of a certain ethnic group or with certain political or religious beliefs

charter a constitution

The Most Terrible War

World War II caused more destruction than any other war. It was the first war in which people used atomic bombs. About 40 to 50 million people died because of the war. Many people had run away from their homes. As a result there were huge numbers of **refugees** in many countries. The atomic bombs dropped on the Japanese cities of Hiroshima and Nagasaki killed more than 100,000 people right away. Thousands of others suffered burns, radiation sickness, and illnesses such as cancer. However, nothing so horrified the world as the discovery of the Nazi **concentration camps.** Nazi Germany killed millions of people in these camps. They also forced people to work in terrible conditions. Most of these people were Jews. Nazi leaders had a plan called the "Final Solution." The goal of the Final Solution was to get rid of all Jewish people in Europe. Most historians think at least 6 million Jews were killed. This event became known as the Holocaust.

New Beginnings

United States President Franklin D. Roosevelt and others believed that an international peacekeeping organization was needed. On April 25, 1945, the Allies formed the United Nations, or UN. The UN is a group whose goal is to keep peace. It is made up of countries from all over the world. At the first meeting the members wrote a **charter,** or constitution. Eleanor Roosevelt represented the United States at this meeting. She was the wife of President Roosevelt, who had just died. Mrs. Roosevelt was in charge of the group that wrote the *Universal Declaration of Human Rights.* This document set the guidelines for human rights. Nations and rulers follow these guidelines to this day. The Allies put war criminals from Germany and Japan on trial. Europe's economies needed to rebuild. Congress passed the Marshall Plan. Under this plan the United States sent $13 billion to Europe. Within a few years the economies of Western Europe were doing well again. But countries in Eastern Europe did not accept the money. Soviet leader Stalin forced them not to. Stalin controlled these countries. He did not want them depending on the United States. Anne Frank was a Jewish girl from the Netherlands. She and her family hid from the Nazis during the war. Anne kept a diary about her thoughts and experiences. The Nazis sent her and her family to concentration camps. Her diary was found later. Her words gave hope to many people.

© Scott Foresman 6

Lesson 3: Review

1. 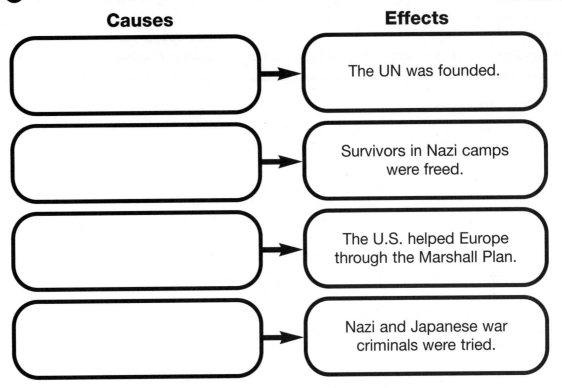 **Cause and Effect** Fill in the chart below by listing the cause of each of the effects listed.

Causes   **Effects**

	The UN was founded.
	Survivors in Nazi camps were freed.
	The U.S. helped Europe through the Marshall Plan.
	Nazi and Japanese war criminals were tried.

2. What ill effects did survivors of the atomic bombings in Nagasaki and Hiroshima suffer?

_____

_____

3. Who was Anne Frank?

_____

_____

4. How did the United Nations give hope to the world?

_____

_____

5. **Critical Thinking:** *Evaluate Information* Why do you think Stalin did not want the Eastern European countries to take advantage of the Marshall Plan?

_____

_____

Lesson 1: The Soviets Advance

Vocabulary

> **nuclear** atomic weapons
> **containment** a policy to stop the spread of communism to other countries

New Superpowers

After World War II the Soviet Union and the United States were "superpowers." This means they were the strongest countries in the world. During the war Allied leaders agreed to let Eastern European countries rule themselves. But by 1948 the Soviet leader Stalin forced communism onto these countries. The Soviet Union controlled Eastern Europe. Winston Churchill said that communist leaders created an "iron curtain." He meant that they put up a wall between Eastern Europe and the West. The wall stopped trade and travel. After the war there was a lot of tension between the Soviet Union and the United States. People called this tension the Cold War. The Cold War was a war of words and threats. Both countries threatened to use **nuclear,** or atomic weapons, against each other.

A Divided Europe

After the war the Allies each took over a part of Germany. Each also controlled a part of Berlin, the German capital. In 1948 Stalin tried to push the French, Americans, and British out of Berlin. He closed off all traffic coming into their parts of Berlin. The people in these areas faced starvation. President Truman responded with the Berlin airlift. He delivered supplies such as food by airplane to the French, British, and American zones of Berlin. Stalin gave up. President Truman worked to stop communism from spreading to other countries. This was called a policy of **containment.** In 1947 the Soviet Union tried to pressure Turkey and Greece into becoming communist. President Truman told these countries that the United States would help them stay free. This promise was known as the Truman Doctrine. The United

States and other countries formed the North Atlantic Treaty Organization, or NATO. Members of NATO made a promise to each other. They promised that if one member were threatened by the Soviets, the others would come to its aid. The Soviet Union formed its own alliance. It was called the Warsaw Pact. It protected the communist countries of Eastern Europe. In 1949 the Western nations joined their zones of occupation to form West Germany. The Soviets formed East Germany from their zone.

The Nuclear Arms Race

The United States and the Soviet Union raced to develop more powerful weapons. In 1949 the Soviet Union tested its first atomic bomb. In the early 1950s, the United States developed a more powerful bomb. It was called the hydrogen bomb, or H-bomb. Soon the Soviets had their own H-bomb. Both countries threatened to destroy each other with these weapons.

The Cuban Missile Crisis

A new leader took over the Soviet Union. He was named Nikita Khrushchev. In 1961 many people from East Germany escaped to West Germany. To stop them Khrushchev built the Berlin Wall. It ran through the middle of Berlin. In October 1962 the United States and the Soviet Union came close to nuclear war. The United States had discovered that the Soviets were building missile bases in Cuba. Cuba is only 90 miles from Florida. President John F. Kennedy wanted to keep Soviet missiles out of Cuba. He used force to stop ships from delivering missiles to Cuba. After a few tense and frightening days, the danger of a nuclear war passed. This event became known as the Cuban missile crisis.

Lesson 1: Review

1. 🔄 **Cause and Effect** Fill in the chart below by listing three causes of the Cold War.

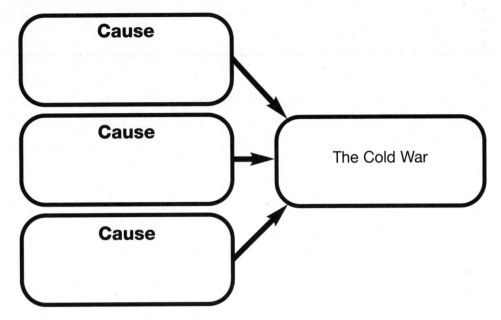

2. What was the purpose of the Berlin airlift?

_____

_____

3. What was the central issue of the Cuban missile crisis?

_____

_____

4. Why did Churchill's term, "the iron curtain," seem to sum up the situation in Europe during the Cold War so well?

_____

_____

5. **Critical Thinking:** *Make Inferences* How was the founding of NATO an effect of Stalin's attempt to take over Berlin? Explain.

_____

_____

Lesson 2: Communism in China

Vocabulary

proletarian of the working class

A Struggle for Control of China

In 1911 a revolution started in China. China's emperor was forced out. China became a republic. A republic does not have a king or an emperor. Sun Yat-sen was a leader of this revolution. He started the Guomindang, or the Nationalist Party. The other political party in China was the Communist Party. Mao Zedong was the leader of the communists. In the 1930s the Nationalist Party ruled most of China. It wanted to get rid of the communists. But the communists escaped to northwest China. Their journey became known as "The Long March." After World War II, the Nationalist Party and the communists fought a civil war. The communists won and took over China in 1949. The nationalists ran away to Taiwan. Taiwan is a small island near China.

The People's Republic of China

The communists set up the People's Republic of China. The nationalists set up a government on Taiwan. China formed an alliance with the Soviet Union. China's leader, Mao, and the communists made many changes in China. They made everyday life easier, especially for the poor. They also united the country. However, Mao took away many freedoms from the people. The Chinese people no longer had freedom of speech or religion. The government also invaded Tibet, a country to the southwest. Mao had a plan to make China more modern. It was called "The Great Leap Forward." He turned China's farms into collectives. But the farms were run poorly. The people starved. There were problems between Taiwan and China. China claimed to own Taiwan. Taiwan felt it was independent. In 1972 U.S. President Richard Nixon visited Mao in China. He hoped to improve relations

between the United States and China. China also had conflicts with the Soviet Union.

The Cultural Revolution

In 1966 Mao started a new revolution in China. He called it the "Great Proletarian Cultural Revolution." **Proletarian** means "of the working class." The revolution became known as the Cultural Revolution. Mao wanted to rid China of all "counter-revolutionary" elements. By this he meant any people with wealth or special privileges. He wanted everybody in China to be equal. Mao's wife, Jiang Qing, helped him do this. Jiang Qing was one of the most powerful people in China during the Cultural Revolution. Mao wanted young people to join the Revolution. Millions of students joined the "Red Guards." They marched in the streets. They attacked anybody who had a high standard of living. This included teachers and older people. They also attacked people who did not agree with the Red Guards. One of these people was Nien Cheng. The Red Guards put her in prison because she was wealthy and privileged. Many others died.

The Last Years

The Cultural Revolution lasted ten years. Many schools were closed. Students were sent to work on farms. Mao's army took over China. The Cultural Revolution ended when Mao died in 1976. Later Jiang Qing was put on trial and sent to prison. Leaders with different ideas took over China.

© Scott Foresman 6

Lesson 2: Review

1. ↻ **Cause and Effect** Fill in the chart below by listing the cause and effects.

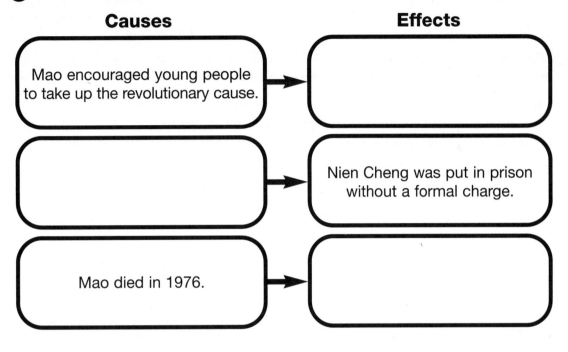

Causes

Mao encouraged young people to take up the revolutionary cause.

Mao died in 1976.

Effects

Nien Cheng was put in prison without a formal charge.

2. What political parties fought for control of China during the civil war of the late 1940s?

_____

_____

3. Who was Jiang Qing and what was her role in China's history?

_____

_____

4. What details can you provide to support the statement "The twentieth century was an era of revolution in China"?

_____

_____

5. **Critical Thinking:** *Detect Bias* Do you think you could believe everything the communist leaders in Beijing said about the government of Taiwan? Could you believe everything Taiwan's leaders said about the People's Republic of China? Explain your answer.

_____

_____

Lesson 3: The Cold War Heats Up

Vocabulary

guerrilla a group of fighters who attack their enemy and then run
détente when tensions between countries are relaxed

The Korean War

Korea had been a divided country since World War II. North Korea was controlled by communists. South Korea was controlled by non-communists. In June 1950 communist North Korea invaded South Korea. The United Nations agreed to send an army to stop the invasion. The United States provided most of the troops and supplies. The UN troops drove the North Koreans out of South Korea. The UN troops pushed them very close to the Chinese border. The Chinese sent troops into North Korea. They pushed the UN forces back. In 1953 North Korea agreed to stop fighting. But North Korea and South Korea never signed a treaty to end the war.

The Vietnam War

The United States worried about the spread of communism in Asia. The Asian country of Vietnam was a lot like Korea. It was divided. North Vietnam was communist. South Vietnam was non-communist. Unlike Korea, North Vietnam had a group of **guerrillas.** They were called the Viet Cong. The Viet Cong and North Vietnam wanted to bring communism to South Vietnam. U.S. President Dwight D. Eisenhower promised to protect South Vietnam. He sent advisers to strengthen South Vietnam's military. But South Vietnam's government was losing control of the country to the Viet Cong. The United States began bombing North Vietnam from airplanes. It sent thousands of troops to help fight the Viet Cong. The war continued. The United States then sent hundreds of thousands of troops. Many died. But the communist fighters kept fighting. People in the United States began to speak out against the war. President Johnson said the United States had to fight because of the domino effect. The

domino effect occurs when dominoes are lined up and one domino falls. It knocks over another domino, until all the dominoes have fallen. President Johnson believed that if South Vietnam became communist, so would all of the other Asian countries. In October 1967, 50,000 people marched to Washington to protest the war.

The War's Final Chapter

In 1968 the Viet Cong and North Vietnamese began the Tet Offensive. It was a series of battles across South Vietnam. The Tet Offensive showed the United States that it would not be able to defeat the North Vietnamese easily. Many people became angry with President Johnson. He decided not to run for president again. Richard Nixon became president in 1969. Nixon wanted the United States to be less involved in the war. He had a plan called Vietnamization. This plan would turn over most of the ground fighting to the South Vietnamese army. The United States continued to bomb North Vietnam. The United States also began fighting in Cambodia, which is next to South Vietnam. Many more protests against the war occurred in the United States. In January 1973 the United States and North Vietnam stopped fighting. But the war between North and South Vietnam continued. In April 1975 North Vietnam took over South Vietnam. Some Americans thought that the United States had fought for nothing. Also the domino effect did not occur. Most of the other countries in Asia stayed non-communist. After the Vietnam War, the U.S. government started a period of **détente.** During this period relations got better with China and the Soviet Union.

© Scott Foresman 6

Lesson 3: Review

1. 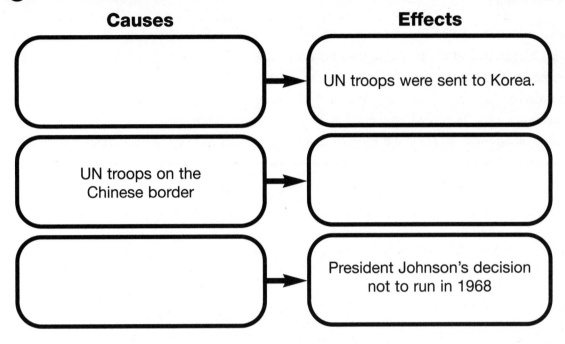 **Cause and Effect** Fill in the chart below by listing a cause or effect.

Causes	Effects

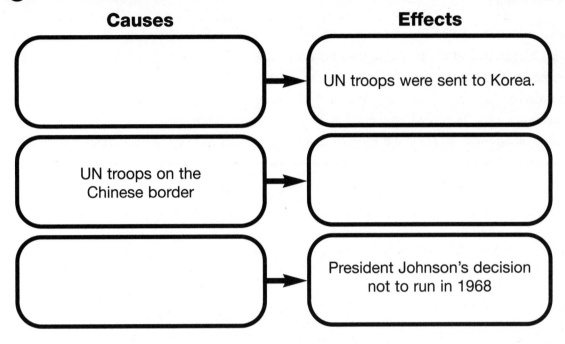

2. How did President Eisenhower help the government of South Vietnam fight against the Communists?

_____

_____

3. How did U.S. involvement in the war change under President Nixon?

_____

_____

4. How were the wars in Korea and Vietnam different from other disagreements with communist countries during the Cold War?

_____

_____

5. **Critical Thinking: *Make Inferences*** What events in other parts of the world would have convinced people that the domino effect would occur if Vietnam became a communist country?

_____

_____

© Scott Foresman 6

Lesson 1: Independence

Vocabulary

decolonization the process of removing colonial rule, or control by another country

coup d'état overthrow of a country's government

segregate to separate

apartheid a system of laws separating black people from white people

sanction a penalty placed on a country by one or more countries

civil disobedience a nonviolent form of protest; the refusal to obey or cooperate with unfair laws

Decolonization

After World War II, nations in Africa began to fight for **decolonization.** They wanted to rule themselves. Ghana fought for its independence in the 1950s. After 1960 decolonization occurred all over Africa. Nations won independence in different ways. Algeria and Kenya fought to gain freedom. By the mid-1970s, most of Africa was independent.

Challenges

Many independent African nations had trouble setting up strong governments. The Congo won independence from Belgium. In 1965 Mobutu Sese Seko led a **coup d'état** against the new Congo government. This means he forced out the government and took power.

Southern Africa

Southern Rhodesia was a British colony in southern Africa. During the 1960s many blacks in Rhodesia began fighting against the white government. In 1965 whites in Rhodesia declared independence from Great Britain. In 1980 blacks won control of the government. Southern Rhodesia became known as Zimbabwe. In 1948 a white government in South Africa passed laws to **segregate,** or separate, blacks from whites. The system of laws was called **apartheid.** Nelson Mandela, a black South African leader, spoke out against apartheid. Many others used nonviolent civil disobedience and protested against apartheid. In the 1980s many Western countries placed **sanctions,** or penalties, on South Africa.

A New Era

In 1990 South Africa's government realized that the sanctions were hurting the country. It also worried that apartheid would cause a civil war. In 1994 black South Africans won the right to vote. They elected Nelson Mandela president.

East and Southeast Asia

Nations in East and Southeast Asia won freedom in different ways. Vietnamese communists forced France to give up Indochina (Vietnam) in 1954. Most British lands in Southeast Asia won independence after World War II. In 1945 Indonesia won a war of independence against the Dutch. In 1997 Great Britain gave Hong Kong to China. In 1999 Portugal turned over the colony of Macao to China. European imperialism in Asia was over.

The Indian Subcontinent

India was a British colony. Many Indians were against British rule. Around 1920 Mohandas Gandhi became the leader of India's independence movement. He believed that the British could control India only if the Indians cooperated. Gandhi protested for freedom in a peaceful way. This form of protest became known as **civil disobedience.**

India Divides

India gained independence through nonviolent civil disobedience on August 14, 1947. On the same day, the Muslim nation of Pakistan was formed out of part of India. In 1971 East Pakistan broke away from West Pakistan. It formed the nation of Bangladesh.

Lesson 1: Review

1. 🔄 **Draw Conclusions** Fill in the missing facts.

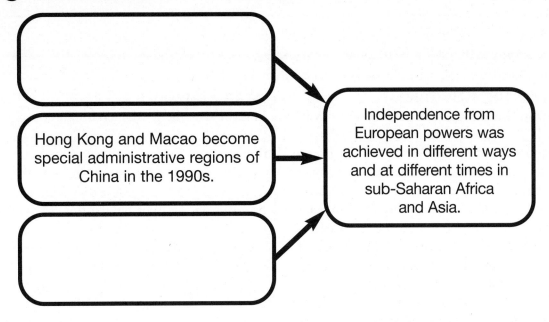

2. How did black South Africans and Western countries react to apartheid?

_____

_____

3. Why did Gandhi believe that nonviolent civil disobedience was the way to gain independence for India?

_____

_____

4. Name four new nations that have formed in Asia and sub-Saharan Africa since World War II.

_____

_____

5. **Critical Thinking:** *Fact or Opinion* Turn to page 607 in your textbook. Find one fact and one opinion.

_____

_____

Lesson 2: The Middle East

Vocabulary

Zionism the movement to build a Jewish state in Palestine

A Growing Palestine

Zionism was the movement to build a Jewish state in Palestine. Arabs and Jews lived in Palestine before World War I. They had some small conflicts. But they usually got along peacefully. Jews were treated badly in Europe in the 1930s. This caused more Jews to leave for Palestine. But the largest number of Jews moved to Palestine because of the Holocaust. This large migration caused problems between Jews and Arabs in Palestine. Great Britain governed Palestine after World War I. The British supported the establishment of a Jewish homeland in Palestine. Great Britain asked the United Nations (UN) for help with the growing conflict in Palestine. The UN wanted to divide Palestine into two states. One state would be an Arab state. The other would be a Jewish state.

State of Israel

British troops left Palestine in 1948. David Ben-Gurion was the Jewish leader. He declared that the Jewish part of Palestine was now the state of Israel. But Arab nations did not recognize Israel as a nation. They did not think that Palestine should be divided. War broke out between Arabs and Jews. The countries of Syria, Egypt, and Jordan joined forces with the Palestinian Arabs, or Palestinians. By 1949 Israel and these Arab countries agreed to stop fighting. Israel took control of a large amount of land in Palestine. This was part of the land that the UN put aside for an Arab state. Thousands of Palestinian Arabs fled. More fighting was to come. This fighting became known as the Arab-Israeli conflict.

Arab States

In the 1950s the British controlled the Suez Canal in Egypt. Gamal Abdel Nasser was the leader of Egypt. He wanted the British to leave his country. His troops blocked the canal. In 1956 France, Great Britain, and Israel invaded Egypt. They wanted to control the Suez Canal. Many Arabs supported Nasser's actions. No Arab leader in the Middle East had ever before stood up to Western nations. Nasser's goal of Arab nationalism, or unity, spread across the Middle East.

Continuing Conflict

Israel and its Arab neighbors continued to fight wars. In 1967 the Six-Day War began. Israel won control of Palestine. It controlled the Gaza Strip, the West Bank, and other areas. More than 1 million Palestinians lived in the Gaza Strip and West Bank. Many joined the Palestinian Liberation Organization (PLO). The PLO was led by Yasir Arafat. It worked to create a Palestinian state. In 1973 another war began. Arab states attacked Israel. Arab states stopped exporting oil to Western countries that supported Israel. Fighting between Israel and the Palestinians continued during the 1980s.

Toward Peace

Israel and some Arab nations have worked for peace. In 1978 Egypt and Israel signed a peace agreement. It was called the Camp David Accords. Jordan signed a peace treaty with Israel in 1994. In the 1990s Israel and Yasir Arafat signed the Oslo Accords. These agreements tried to end the Arab-Israeli conflict. But violence continues between Arabs and Israelis.

© Scott Foresman 6

Lesson 2: Review

1. ↻ **Draw Conclusions** Write a conclusion about how the state of Israel was created using the given clues.

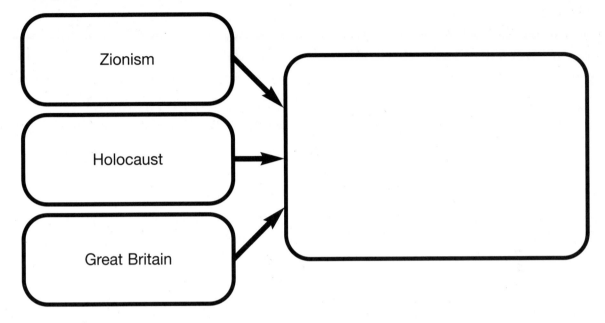

2. How did Arab nationalism affect the Middle East?

_____

_____

3. What was the result of the UN plan to divide Palestine into Jewish and Arab states?

_____

_____

4. How did Arab hopes for independence and Jewish hopes for a homeland in Palestine cause tension?

_____

_____

5. **Critical Thinking:** *Evaluate Information* In the Oslo Accords, Israel agreed to give land back to the Palestinians. The Palestinians then agreed to recognize Israel. Do you think this is a fair trade? Explain.

_____

_____

Lesson 3: Eastern Europe

Vocabulary

dissident person who protests against a government

perestroika Gorbachev's program to reform the Soviet economy

glasnost Gorbachev's policy to allow Soviet people some freedom of speech

Changes in Eastern Europe

In November 1989 the gates of the Berlin Wall were opened. People could now move between East Germany and West Germany. Then East Germany's communist government fell. In 1990 East Germany and West Germany became one country again. By 1991 the Berlin Wall was destroyed. All of the events that ended communism in Eastern Europe became known as the "Revolution of 1989." After World War II, the Soviets had forced many Eastern European countries to have communist governments. In the 1950s the countries of East Germany, Hungary, and Czechoslovakia began to rebel. The Soviet Army used force to stop the rebellions. Things began to change in 1980. The Polish government accepted a labor union that was controlled by workers. Lech Walesa led the union. Before this the government controlled all labor unions. Mikhail Gorbachev was the Soviet leader. He called for more freedom in Eastern Europe. Many Eastern European countries broke free from communist rule. In 1990 Lech Walesa was elected president of Poland. Vaclav Havel became president of Czechoslovakia. He had been a **dissident,** or protester against the government. Czechoslovakia later split into the Czech Republic and the Slovak Republic. Yugoslavia also broke apart after the fall of communism. The end of communism in Yugoslavia helped form the nations of Slovenia, Croatia, Bosnia and Herzegovina, and Macedonia.

Communism Crumbles

During the Cold War, the Soviet Union spent a lot of money on weapons. The nation had little money left over for other things. Many Soviet people were unhappy with the communist system. In the mid-1980s, Mikhail Gorbachev led the Communist Party. He began *perestroika.* Gorbachev used this policy to reform the Soviet economy. He also started *glasnost.* This policy gave the Soviet people some freedom of speech. Gorbachev wanted the Soviet Union to become a democracy. In the 1990s Soviet republics began declaring independence. Some Soviet leaders were unhappy with this. They blamed Gorbachev. In August 1991 they tried to overthrow Gorbachev's government. Boris Yeltsin helped stop the rebellion. In December 1991 Yeltsin and other leaders declared the end of the Soviet Union. Yeltsin also ended communism. Fifteen new nations formed from the breakup of the Soviet Union.

Lesson 3: Review

1. ⟳ **Draw Conclusions** Fill in the conclusion based on the given facts.

The communist system failed in Eastern Europe, and many people lost faith in communism.

Workers wanted labor unions free of communist control.

Eastern Europeans protested against their governments.

2. What events does "the Revolution of 1989" describe?

_____

_____

3. Why did Gorbachev start the policy of *perestroika?* The policy of *glasnost?*

_____

_____

4. What changes did the end of communism bring to Eastern Europe?

_____

_____

5. **Critical Thinking:** *Make Generalizations* How did the Soviet response to protests in Eastern Europe in the 1950s and 1960s compare to those of Gorbachev in the 1980s?

_____

_____

Lesson 1: Economic Cooperation

Vocabulary

gross domestic product (GDP) a measure of a nation's wealth; it measures the value of all final goods and services produced in a country in a year

trading bloc a group of countries that agree to trade with each other and place lower taxes on trade goods

euro money used by all countries in the European Union

trade agreement rules for trade between countries

Economies Without Borders

We live in a global economy. The products we buy come from all over the world. In a global economy, many countries trade with one another. This trade makes some countries and people rich. But the global economy also increases competition. Competition has forced some industries to shut down. Some countries such as the United States, Japan, and European nations are wealthy. They are called developed nations. Other nations are not as wealthy. They are still developing their economies. These nations are called developing nations. Many developing nations are found in Africa and Asia. We figure out a nation's wealth by its **gross domestic product (GDP).** A nation's GDP is the value of all final goods and services produced in that country in a year.

Trade and Cooperation

Many people believe that free trade between nations leads to peace and wealth. Many nations joined trading blocs to create more trade. A **trading bloc** is a group of countries that agree to trade with lower taxes. The largest trading bloc is the European Union, or EU. The EU began as the European Economic Community. It was created to set up a common market. A common market is an economic union. It is formed to increase trade and cooperation among its members. By 1993, fifteen European countries belonged to the EU. In 1999 the EU created its own money. It is called the **euro.** The euro made trade easier between EU countries. These nations do not

have to change their money every time they want to trade with one another. In 1967 five Southeast Asian countries formed their own trading bloc. It is named the Association of Southeast Asian Nations (ASEAN). Today the members of ASEAN are Myanmar (Burma), Laos, Thailand, Cambodia, Vietnam, the Philippines, Brunei, Malaysia, Singapore, and Indonesia.

American Trading Blocs

Trading blocs developed in North and South America too. In 1991 Argentina, Brazil, Paraguay, and Uruguay formed Mercosur. Mercosur became known as the "Southern Common Market." The United States, Canada, and Mexico set up a trading bloc in 1994. Their agreement is called the North American Free Trade Agreement (NAFTA). A **trade agreement** lists rules for trade between countries. NAFTA must work to remove tariffs on goods made and sold in the United States. The agreement helped trade grow between the United States and Mexico. In 1995 the World Trade Organization (WTO) formed. It helps nations settle conflicts over trade.

© Scott Foresman 6

Lesson 1: Review

1. **Cause and Effect** Write in the missing cause and effect.

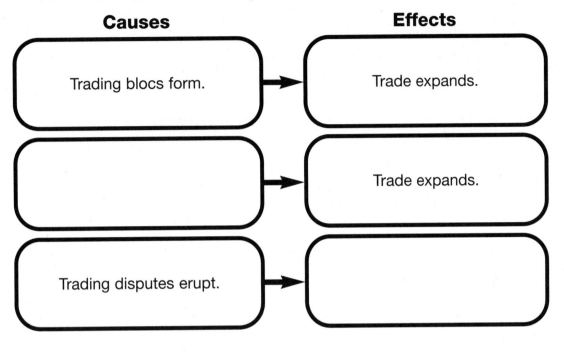

Causes   **Effects**

Trading blocs form. → Trade expands.

[   ] → Trade expands.

Trading disputes erupt. → [   ]

2. Define *gross domestic product.*

_____

_____

3. Name four trading blocs and list their members. Use the map on page 632 of your textbook.

_____

_____

4. Explain the role of the World Trade Organization.

_____

_____

5. **Critical Thinking:** *Make Inferences* What might economic conditions be like in countries that do not belong to trading blocs? Explain your answer.

_____

_____

Lesson 2: Conflicts of Identity

Vocabulary

ethnicity the language, customs, and culture shared by a group

multiethnic nation a nation with many different ethnic groups

ethnic cleansing to drive out or kill people of a certain ethnicity

repressive not allowing someone to have basic human rights, such as freedom of speech

Identity and Ethnicity

People who have the same **ethnicity** share a language, customs, and culture. Sometimes wars are fought because of ethnicity. Yugoslavia was a **multiethnic** nation. This means it had many different ethnic groups. Yugoslavia had many republics. Yugoslavia began to break apart after communism ended in Eastern Europe. In 1991 Slovenia and Croatia, two of its republics, declared independence. Serbia and Croatia fought a civil war. Different ethnic groups fought each other.

Kosovo

The republic of Bosnia and Herzegovina declared independence in 1992. Serbians practiced ethnic cleansing against the people of Bosnia and Herzegovina. **Ethnic cleansing** means to drive out or kill people of a certain ethnicity. Thousands of people were forced out of Bosnia and Herzegovina. Then fighting began in a part of Serbia called Kosovo. Many people in Kosovo were Muslim Albanians. They were called Kosovars. The Kosovars wanted independence. Serbian soldiers killed thousands of Kosovars and forced many people out of Kosovo.

Central Africa

Rwanda and Burundi are countries in central Africa. They fought a civil war in the 1990s. The fighting was between the Tutsi and Hutu ethnic groups. In 1993 the Tutsi army killed thousands of Hutu citizens in Burundi. The next year the Hutu killed many Tutsi in Rwanda. Many villages and cities in Rwanda and Burundi are destroyed. Many people lost their homes and are hungry.

Northern Ireland

People also fight wars over religion. In the 1920s Great Britain divided Ireland. Northern Ireland stayed part of the United Kingdom. The rest of Ireland became an independent republic. In Northern Ireland most people are Protestants. In the rest of Ireland most people are Catholics. In the late 1960s, Catholics in Northern Ireland began fighting for civil rights. The conflict grew.

The Struggle of Women

In many countries women do not have the same rights as men. In 1996 the Taliban took power in Afghanistan. The Taliban is a religious political party. The Taliban did not allow women to go to school or work.

Struggles for Change

Some nations have repressive governments. A **repressive** government does not allow its citizens to have basic human rights. Aung San Suu Kyi has fought for human rights in Myanmar (Burma). In 1994 people in Chiapas, Mexico, rebelled against their government. Many farmers had lost their land. They also wanted more say in government. Some changes have been made.

Limited Freedom

The People's Republic of China is another country that limits its citizens' freedom. The government has started to give people more freedom. For example, people can start their own businesses. But the government does not give people other human rights.

Lesson 2: Review

1. **Draw Conclusions** Write a conclusion based on the given facts.

The Bosnians and Kosovars have different ethnic identities.

Protestants and Catholics have different religious identities.

The Hutu and Tutsi have different traditions.

2. What caused thousands of refugees to flee Bosnia and Herzegovina in the 1990s?

_____

_____

3. How are the situations in central Africa and Northern Ireland alike and different?

_____

_____

4. Name three places in the world where people have been struggling for freedom or human rights.

_____

_____

5. **Critical Thinking: *Detect Bias*** Do you think countries that do not give equal status to men and women are showing a bias? Why or why not?

_____

_____

Lesson 3: Political Conflicts and Challenges

Vocabulary

terrorism the use of violence and fear to achieve political goals

International Struggles

Terrorism is the use of violence and fear to achieve political goals. Terrorism is often used against ordinary people. Many people have worked to stop terrorism. In the twentieth century, the number of international terrorist attacks increased. More terrorist groups used violence to try to reach their political goals. In 1914 a member of a terrorist group killed Austrian Archduke Franz Ferdinand. This event led to World War I.

Terrorism Against Americans

Terrorism against Americans is not new. In the late eighteenth century, pirates from the Barbary Islands attacked U.S. trade ships in the Mediterranean Sea. President Thomas Jefferson sent naval ships to stop the attacks. By the twentieth century, terrorists began to attack ordinary people as well as the military. In 1983 a bomb exploded at the U.S. embassy in Lebanon. Then a bomb destroyed an American airplane over Lockerbie, Scotland. In 1995 a truck bomb exploded outside the Murrah Federal Building in Oklahoma. In 1998 bombs exploded outside U.S. embassies in Africa. But the worst terrorist attacks occurred on September 11, 2001. That morning terrorists hijacked, or took over, four American airplanes. They crashed two of the planes into the twin towers of the World Trade Center in New York City. Thousands of people died. The towers were completely destroyed. The third plane crashed into the Pentagon in Arlington, Virginia. The fourth plane crashed

in Pennsylvania. The American people responded to the attacks with courage. Rescue workers risked their lives to save people. Many people donated blood. Others gave money to help the victims. Congress passed stronger laws against terrorism. Security increased at airports, skyscrapers, train and bus stations, and other public buildings. The United States had evidence that the Taliban government in Afghanistan was protecting the terrorist group responsible for the attacks. On October 7, 2001, the United States and Great Britain began bombing Taliban sites in Afghanistan. By December, Taliban rule of Afghanistan was over. Efforts to set up a new government had begun.

Working Together

Countries all over the world work to end terrorism. Many work together to bring about peace. Many acts of terrorism are caused by differences. These differences may be in religion, ethnicity, or political beliefs. For example there is conflict between Protestants and Catholics in Northern Ireland. This conflict has led to terrorist attacks. Terrorist attacks also have occurred because of fighting between Jews and Arabs in the Middle East. People have formed groups to bring people together. They want to show that different groups of people can work together for peace and understanding.

© Scott Foresman 6

Lesson 3: Review

1. **Draw Conclusions** Fill in the missing facts that support the conclusion.

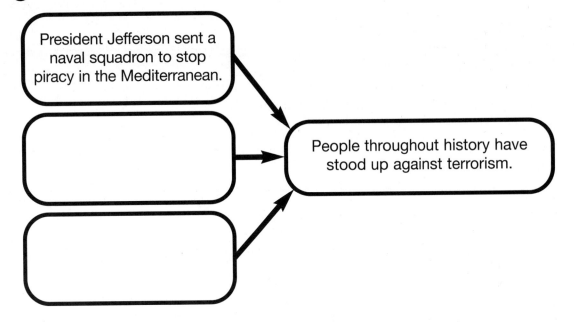

2. What is terrorism and when is it used?

_____

_____

3. How has the United States responded to acts of terrorism?

_____

_____

4. How have people around the world responded to acts of terrorism?

_____

_____

5. **Critical Thinking:** *Solve Complex Problems* What can governments around the world do to stand up to terrorists and terrorism?

_____

_____

_____

Lesson 1: Population Growth and Change

Vocabulary

millennium one thousand years

megacity a city region with a population of more than 10 million people

demographer a scientist who studies population trends

immigration when people move to a new country to stay permanently or for a long time

zero population growth a balanced population in which just enough babies are being born to replace people who have died

Population Growth

A **millennium** is a thousand years. At the start of the second millennium, the population of Earth was 6 billion people. In the late twentieth century, Mexico City, Mexico, was the city with the biggest population in the world. Many people are moving to urban, or city, areas. There often are more jobs in cities than in rural, or country, areas. But many cities are growing so fast that they cannot provide enough housing or clean water for the people who live there. A **megacity** is a city region with 10 million or more people. Calcutta, India, is a megacity. It is one of the world's poorest cities.

Population Movement

In the late 1800s, people began to move from the country to the city. By the 1960s people in developing countries began to move to developed countries. There is not enough housing, water, or jobs for the people who live in many developing nations. The population is growing much faster in developing nations than in most developed nations. Madagascar is a developing nation near Africa. The population in Madagascar will double in less than 25 years. The population also is growing quickly in Guatemala, Ethiopia, and the Philippines. Some developed nations such as Japan, Italy, and Sweden are barely growing at all.

Immigration

Some scientists study population trends, or patterns. They are called **demographers.** Many demographers believe that population growth depends on the status of women. In developed countries more women have the chance to go to school. Educated women usually have fewer children. In developing countries fewer women have the chance to go to school or to work. **Immigration** is the process of people moving to a new country to stay permanently or for a long time. Immigration from developing countries is changing the cultures of developed nations. For example many people from North Africa have immigrated to France. Most of these immigrants are Muslims. These people brought their food and religion with them. Now many other people in France eat food dishes from Arab countries and are Muslims.

A Population Explosion?

Demographers used to think that a "population explosion" was going to occur. They worried that too many people would be born. Today some demographers think population growth is slowing. In some developed countries, there is **zero population growth.** This means that there are just enough babies being born to replace people who have died. In developing nations and cities, growing populations are still a problem.

© Scott Foresman 6

Lesson 1: Review

1. 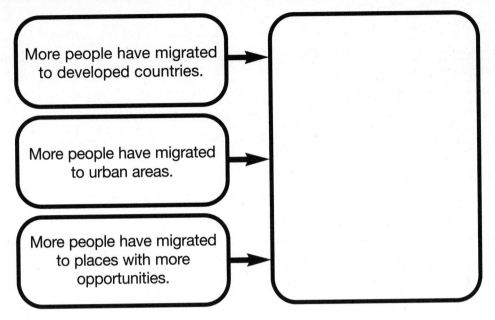 **Draw Conclusions** Write a conclusion based on the facts in the diagram.

2. Why are people moving to cities?

   _____

   _____

3. In which parts of the world is the population growing the fastest?

   _____

   _____

4. Name one challenge that population movement presents.

   _____

   _____

5. **Critical Thinking:** *Make Generalizations* How does immigration affect populations in developed and developing countries?

   _____

   _____

   _____

Lesson 2: Earth's Environment

Vocabulary

global warming a slow increase in the average temperature of Earth's surface

carbon dioxide a gas that is produced by burning gasoline or other fuels; it traps heat in Earth's atmosphere

greenhouse effect the process by which trapped heat warms Earth's atmosphere

pesticide a chemical used to kill pests such as insects

environmentalist a person who works to protect Earth's natural environment

endangered species animals and plants that could die out

deforestation the process of cutting down forests

desertification the process of turning fertile land into dry, useless land

pollution the process of making the environment dirty

The Environment

Global warming is a slow increase in the average temperature of Earth's surface. Scientists do not agree on why global warming is happening. Many believe that a gas called **carbon dioxide** is helping to cause it. Human activities may increase levels of carbon dioxide. People help produce carbon dioxide when they burn fuel. Carbon dioxide traps heat that is given off by Earth. This trapped heat warms the atmosphere. This process is called the **greenhouse effect.** The amount of carbon dioxide in the atmosphere has gone up since the mid-1800s. In the 1960s more people realized that their actions affect the environment. In 1962 a scientist named Rachel Carson wrote *Silent Spring*. This book described how **pesticides** were killing birds and other animals. Because of this book, some people became **environmentalists.** These people took action to protect the environment. They worked to pass environmental laws. In 1970 Congress set up the Environmental Protection Agency. This agency makes sure groups and people do not harm the environment. Congress passed laws to protect **endangered species.** In Europe "green" political parties formed. They worked to pass laws to protect the environment.

Problems and Solutions

In 1997 leaders from more than 160 countries met in Kyoto, Japan. They created a global warming treaty. The treaty asked countries to lower their production of carbon dioxide and other harmful gases. But most countries have not signed the treaty. They are afraid it will harm their economies. Another problem is feeding the world's growing population. Many farmers have cut down forests to grow more crops. This process is called **deforestation.** Deforestation adds to global warming. This is because trees absorb carbon dioxide. When trees are cut down, more carbon dioxide can get into the atmosphere. People plant new trees to work against deforestation. Land also has been changed by **desertification.** In this process fertile land dries up. This sometimes happens when farmers plow fields and animals overgraze the land. The topsoil becomes loose and dry. Then it blows away. **Pollution** is the process of making the environment dirty. Garbage is a common form of pollution. People recycle aluminum, paper, and glass to lower the amount of garbage produced.

Lesson 2: Review

1. **Cause and Effect** Fill in the empty effects boxes.

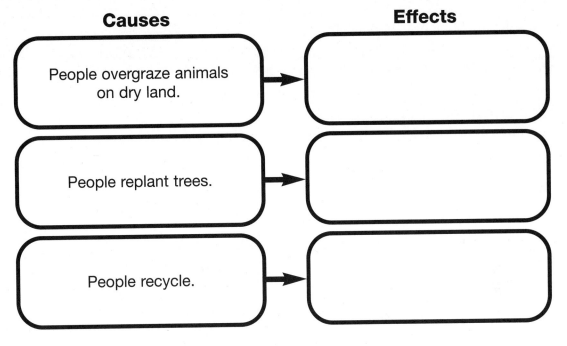

Causes

Effects

People overgraze animals on dry land.	→	
People replant trees.	→	
People recycle.	→	

2. What is an environmentalist?

_____

_____

3. What has happened to the amount of carbon dioxide in Earth's atmosphere?

_____

_____

4. How have people helped to solve environmental problems in the last 50 years?

_____

_____

5. **Critical Thinking:** *Evaluate Information* Do you think that humans have done more good or harm to Earth? Why or why not?

_____

_____

Lesson 3: Energy

Vocabulary

conservation limiting our use of energy

fossil fuel a fuel that formed long ago, deep inside the earth

nonrenewable resource a resource that cannot be easily replaced

renewable resource a resource that cannot be used up easily

hydroelectric energy energy from water power

geothermal energy energy from super-hot water underground

Using Energy

People use a lot of energy. Energy is produced from natural resources. Supplying people with the energy they need and want is a big challenge. We must find new energy sources. We also must learn to use less energy. Limiting our use of energy is called **conservation.** Conservation can help us solve our energy problems. Electricity comes from power plants. We use coal, petroleum (oil), and natural gas to run power plants. These natural resources are called **fossil fuels.** Fossil fuels formed deep in the earth a long time ago. They are **nonrenewable resources.** This means that once they are gone they cannot be easily replaced. Scientists think oil will be the first fossil fuel to run out.

Meeting Energy Needs

Much of the world's oil is found in the Middle East. In 1973 many countries in this region cut their production of oil. They formed the Organization of Petroleum Exporting Countries (OPEC). They raised oil prices. This caused an oil crisis all over the world. The United States depends on OPEC for much of its oil. The United States is looking for ways to meet its own energy needs. Fossil fuels, including oil, give off carbon dioxide. This may cause global warming. Nuclear power is a nonrenewable resource that does not give off carbon dioxide. Nuclear power could provide energy for thousands of years. But there can be problems with nuclear power.

Radioactive, or nuclear, gases can make people sick or die. Nuclear power produces radioactive waste. It must be buried deep underground.

Alternative Energy

People also use alternative, or other, energy sources to meet their energy needs. **Renewable resources** provide people with energy. Solar energy, water, and wind are examples of renewable resources. Some power plants use wind power from windmills to make energy. Others use water power from rapidly flowing rivers. This energy is called **hydroelectric energy.** Waterfalls such as Niagara Falls are a great source of hydroelectric energy. **Geothermal energy** comes from super-hot water underground. Scientists also are trying to find new ways to make energy. One example is nuclear fusion. Nuclear fusion produces energy by combining atoms. Scientists also are making cars and trucks that use less energy.

© Scott Foresman 6

Lesson 3: Review

1. ⟳ **Draw Conclusions** Write a conclusion based on the given facts.

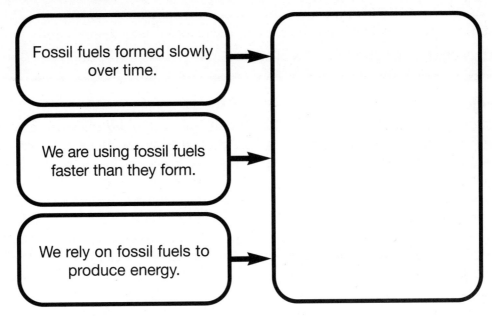

Fossil fuels formed slowly over time. →

We are using fossil fuels faster than they form. →

We rely on fossil fuels to produce energy. →

2. What are fossil fuels and which one will probably run out first?

_____

_____

3. List a benefit and a disadvantage of nuclear energy.

_____

_____

4. Identify alternative energy sources we use today.

_____

_____

5. **Critical Thinking:** *Solve Complex Problems* Make a list of the qualities a good energy source has.

_____

_____

© Scott Foresman 6

Lesson 4: Technology

Vocabulary

space station a large satellite that people use as a scientific base
satellite a human-made object sent into space

New Technology

A **space station** is a large satellite. A **satellite** is a human-made object that is sent into space. Satellites travel around Earth. People use space stations as scientific bases. Technology involves using knowledge, resources, and tools. We use technology to accomplish or improve something. Technology has allowed us to launch satellites, space stations, and space shuttles into space. In 1957 the former Soviet Union sent the first satellite into space. It was called *Sputnik I.* Today telephones and cable TV depend on satellites. In 1961 the Soviets sent the first human into space. In 1969 the United States sent the first people to the moon.

New Possibilities

Another form of technology developed in the late twentieth century. People began mapping human genes. Genes are the blueprint, or plan, for life. Scientists from all over the world are taking part in the Human Genome Project. They are working to map out all of the more than 30,000 human genes. Understanding the genes will help researchers explain how some diseases develop. This may help scientists cure these diseases. Some people are worried about gene research. They think scientists may use what they learn for purposes other than curing diseases.

Limits

Many scientists today study a disease called Acquired Immunodeficiency Syndrome (AIDS). AIDS is a deadly disease. It attacks a person's immune system. Scientists are using technology to find a cure. Flossie Wong-Staal is a scientist studying AIDS. She worked with a group to discover the human immunodeficiency virus, or HIV. HIV causes AIDS. The work done with AIDS shows that technology can solve some problems. But it also shows that it cannot solve other problems. For example anti-AIDS drugs can keep people with AIDS healthy for many years. But many people do not have enough money to pay for these drugs. This includes many people in developing nations. Leaders are working to raise money to help people with AIDS. Technology cannot solve this problem.

Quick Study

Lesson 4: Review

1. ⟳ **Draw Conclusions** Write a conclusion based on the given facts.

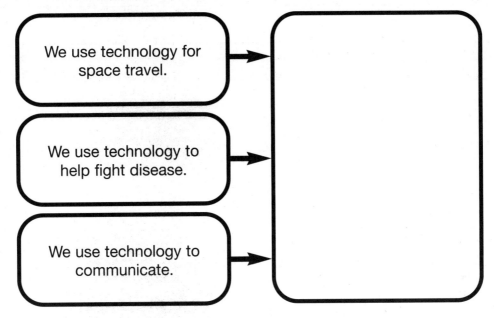

We use technology for space travel.

We use technology to help fight disease.

We use technology to communicate.

2. Explain how we have used technology in space.

_____

_____

3. What is the Human Genome Project?

_____

_____

4. Give an example of a problem that technology might solve and an example of a problem that it cannot solve.

_____

_____

5. **Critical Thinking:** *Evaluate Information* Of the technologies discussed in this lesson, which do you think is most important? Explain your answer.

_____

_____

© Scott Foresman 6

NOTES

NOTES

NOTES

NOTES

NOTES

NOTES

NOTES

NOTES

NOTES

NOTES

NOTES

NOTES

NOTES